EU DIPLOMACY IN MULTILATERAL FORA

This magisterial volume draws on the expertise of leading scholars, practitioners and policy makers to chart the EU's participation in six key international organisations: the UN, the WTO, the ILO, the WHO, the ITU and the FAO. Each is explored from a unique dual perspective: firstly from that of the EU, and secondly from that of the organisation itself. This collection offers a truly innovative approach to ensure a better understanding of the EU's role as a global diplomatic power.

Volume 129 in the Series Modern Studies in European Law

Modern Studies in European Law

Recent titles in this series:

The Future of EU Constitutionalism
Edited by Matej Avbelj

The Changing Role of Citizens in EU Democratic Governance
Edited by Davor Jancic

The EU and the Baltic Sea Area
Edited by Allan Rosas and Henrik Ringbom

The Evolving Governance of EU Competition Law in a Time of Disruptions: A Constitutional Perspective
Edited by Carlo Maria Colombo, Kathryn Wright and Mariolina Eliantonio

The European Integrated Border Management: Frontex, Human Rights, and International Responsibility
Giulia Raimondo

Private Autonomy in EU Internal Market Law: Parameters of its Protection and Limitation
Rufat Babayev

Free Movement and Welfare Access in the European Union: Re-Balancing Conflicting Interests in Citizenship Jurisprudence
Victoria Hooton

EU Trade and Investment Treaty-Making Post-Lisbon: Moving Beyond Mixity
Gesa Kübek

The Normative Foundations for EU Criminal Justice: Powers, Limits and Justifications
Jacob Öberg

EU Neighbourhood Law: Wider Europe and the Extended EU's Legal Space
Alessandro Petti

The Dynamics of Powers in the European Union
Edited by Christina Eckes, Päivi Leino-Sandberg and Anna W Ghavanin

The European Convention on Human Rights and Private Law: Comparative Perspectives from South-Eastern Europe
Edited by Mateja Durovic and Cristina Poncibò

Judging Composite Decision-Making: The Transformation of European Administrative Law
Filipe Brito Bastos

EU Diplomacy in Multilateral Fora
Edited by Christine Kaddous and Frank Hoffmeister

For the complete list of titles in this series
see www.bloomsbury.com/uk/series/modern-studies-in-european-law/

EU Diplomacy in Multilateral Fora

Edited by
Christine Kaddous
and
Frank Hoffmeister

•HART•
OXFORD • LONDON • NEW YORK • NEW DELHI • SYDNEY

HART PUBLISHING

Bloomsbury Publishing Plc

Kemp House, Chawley Park, Cumnor Hill, Oxford, OX2 9PH, UK

1385 Broadway, New York, NY 10018, USA

29 Earlsfort Terrace, Dublin 2, Ireland

HART PUBLISHING, the Hart/Stag logo, BLOOMSBURY and the Diana logo are trademarks of Bloomsbury Publishing Plc

First published in Great Britain 2024

A catalogue record for this book is available from the British Library.

A catalogue record for this book is available from the Library of Congress.

ISBN: HB: 978-1-50996-771-1
ePDF: 978-1-50996-773-5
ePub: 978-1-50996-772-8

Typeset by Compuscript Ltd, Shannon
www.bloomsbury.com

To find out more about our authors and books visit www.hartpublishing.co.uk. Here you will find extracts, author information, details of forthcoming events and the option to sign up for our newsletters.

PREFACE

In May 2022, the Centre d'études juridiques européennes (Centre for European Legal Studies) at the University of Geneva organised an international colloquium on EU diplomacy in multilateral fora within the framework of the EUDIPLO Jean Monnet Network. Encouraged by the success of the previous conference, which had led to the compilation entitled *The European Union in International Organisations and Global Governance* (Oxford, Hart Publishing, 2015), we asked the speakers to turn their highly interesting talks into fully-fledged contributions to this compilation. As a result, we are proud to present the latest insights about the EU's diplomatic record in selected multilateral fora. The overarching idea was to investigate not only the legal status of the European Union, but also its actual influence on the policy-making of the international body in question.

In her opening piece, *Christine Kaddous*, Director of the Geneva Centre for European Legal Studies, recalls the important rules and principles of EU participation in international fora to ensure good governance. She highlights the double challenge for the EU actors in any diplomatic setting. First, their range of activity is set by the formal status of the EU, which can range from membership, through full participant to mere observer status, or no status at all. Second, the internal cohesion is determined by the complex triangle between the European Commission (or the European External Action Service in areas of foreign policy), the Council and the EU Delegation accredited to the international organisation. These actors need to sort out *who* speaks on behalf of the EU (and sometimes its Member States), and *what* the content of such EU intervention should be. *Kaddous* makes the important point that such time-consuming or inconclusive intra-EU discussions may also be one important reason why the EU may sometimes 'punch below its weight' to influence the relevant policy-making at the UN. The author refers to good governance in the EU's participation in international organisations which hinges on coordination and sincere cooperation between EU institutions and Member States.

Josephine Norris and *Flavia Marisi*, both members of the European Commission's Legal Service, offer a detailed analysis of the EU's approach towards WTO reform. Firmly anchored in the Geneva system as a full member, the EU has put forward substantive proposals in all three WTO pillars. With respect to the negotiation function, there is a need to update not only the WTO rulebook to address new issues, but also the method of negotiation. The crucial issue is whether and under what conditions plurilateral agreements may be allowed in the WTO as a suitable way forward when not all WTO members wish to engage. Turning to the monitoring and deliberative function, the authors summarise the EU's proposals to strengthen transparency and put more weight on the notification requirements. Moreover, the EU also propagates reforms on applying Special and Differentiated Treatment wishes to restrict the right of developing countries to self-designate themselves as such. Finally, the authors recall the EU's efforts to keep the appellate system for trade disputes alive by creating an alternative system as long as the Appellate Body remains dysfunctional. In a most innovative chapter, *Norris* and *Marisi* then develop an argument about the EU's influence and how to measure it in the WTO debate at large. They conclude that the EU is arguable uniquely placed to assist in the process of reform. At the same time, it is unclear to them whether the EU's increasingly bilateral approaches may help to build consensus to achieve meaningful reform in the WTO.

The Legal Counsel of the Food and Agriculture Organization (FAO), *Donata Rugaramabu*, presents the participation of the EU and its Member States in this specialised UN organisation located in Rome. As the EU has been a full member of the FAO since 1991, one could expect that the law and practice is settled by now. However, as *Rugaramabu* shows with great insight, the participation and speaking rights of the EU in the FAO Governing Bodies and other statutory bodies do not necessarily give clear guidance on many practical issues, such as seating arrangements. Moreover, the right of the Member State holding the Presidency of the Council to speak for the EU in the FAO Council gave rise to tensions, which were settled by an international legal opinion issued by the FAO Legal Office in 2021. On the policy side, *Rugaramabu* underlines the important role of the EU as a strategic partner and important contributor with reference to recent practice in the field. She concludes with a quote from the FAO Director-General, according to whom the organisation looks forward to continuing its 'close partnership with the European Union, to ensure that FAO remains and further evolves as an efficient, effective and transparent organisation that puts people first, thereby accelerating progress towards achieving the Sustainable Development Goals'.

Maurizio Bussi, the Deputy Regional Director for Europe and Central Asia in the International Labour Organization (ILO), switches the focus to the EU's relationship with one of the oldest international organisations in Geneva. Established in 1919, it is based on an atypical tri-partite structure with representatives of governments, employers and employees. Nevertheless, as early as 1958 the EU tried to work together with the ILO. According to *Bussi*, this first phase of interaction lasted until 1999, when a more intensive collaboration started on the basis of an exchange of letters agreed 10 years before. Hence, from 2000–07, the EU became a sort of 'policy incubator' for the ILO. The third phase, since 2008, sees the two organisations in a strong relationship of mutual consultation and support for their respective policies. The author then paints a very impressive picture of ongoing activities in four areas, namely (i) the EU's support to advance the standard-setting agenda of the ILO, (ii) the integration of international labour standards and technical advice from the ILO into EU policy frameworks, (iii) the EU's financial and technical support for ILO capacity-building efforts in third countries, and (iv) research collaboration in key areas of interest to advance the knowledge frontier.

The Head of the European External Action Service's Legal Department, *Frank Hoffmeister*, continues the analysis on the EU's position in FAO and ILO by adding the intra-EU perspective. He recalls that internal preparation and external representation of EU positions in FAO is still governed by a pre-Lisbon arrangement, which includes the rotating Presidency of the Council as an EU representative. However, since the entry into force of the Lisbon Treaty only the European Commission, the High Representative for Foreign Affairs and Security Policy, and EU Delegations are entitled to represent the EU, unless they nominate other actors as spokespersons. He therefore argues that it is high time to replace the internal arrangements. A more streamlined internal procedure and clear rules on external representation would also allow the EU to increase its influence in the policy-making of the FAO in his view. With respect to the ILO, the EU must ask its Member States to ratify new Conventions on behalf of the EU when the EU wishes to become a party to a given ILO Convention touching upon EU powers. While this topic has been well researched already and led to ECJ jurisprudence, the new element in his contribution is a presentation on how the EU actively tries to foster ILO principles in its Free Trade Agreements with third countries by including innovative chapters on 'trade and sustainable developments' in the standard text of every FTA since 2011. Finally, *Hoffmeister* also analyses the status of the EU in the World Health Organization (WHO). While it is generally treated as an observer only, it has exercised full participant rights when the WHO is negotiating international treaties, which (partially) fall within the powers of the EU. For the author, this model could be extended to other WHO activities as well.

Jan Wouters, Director at the Leuven Centre for Global Governance Studies at the University of Leuven, adds another comparative piece, focusing on EU participation in global economic governance institutions. He starts by giving a fascinating overview over the informal structures such as G7 and G20. As they lack a formal legal statute, much depends on political will and diplomatic practice. Importantly, the EU has managed to secure a strong presence in both fora, but again internal questions of decision-making and external representation are a complicating factor. *Wouters* then presents the case of the EU in the WTO and the OECD as a contrast, where the EU enjoys membership and full participant status. Importantly, he finds that OECD policy and standard-setting initiatives often find their way into EU legislation. Turning to the UN economic bodies (ECOSOC and some subcommittees), *Wouters* argues that the EU is a 'limited actor' there, while he deplores the lack of any status for the EU at all in the Bretton Woods institutions (World Bank and IMF). In conclusion, it is 'most striking' for him that the EU does not have any comprehensive strategy to optimise its scattered presence and role in the various institutions of global economic governance.

The final piece is dedicated to the EU's activities at the UN Human Rights Council (HRC) in Geneva. The former Director for UN affairs at the European External Action Service and now EU Ambassador at the OECD and UNESCO in Paris, *Christina Kokkinakis*, and *Andrej Auersperger Matić*, a member of the EEAS Legal Department, sketch the shaky status of the EU in the main UN human rights body. Since UNGA Resolution 65/276 only applies to the work of the General Assembly, the EU has limited participation rights in the Human Rights Council. The authors argue that these restrictions are not justified anymore and that the working methods in the HRC should follow the established practice of the General Assembly itself. Despite this handicap the EU influence is felt in the daily work of the HRC. *Kokkinakis* and *Matić* present, in particular, the negotiations about a legally binding UN text on supply chain due diligence. While the Council has not entrusted the Commission (yet) with formal negotiation directives, EU representatives closely follow the discussions in Geneva and are even sought after by third parties. The authors find it plausible that the EU will play an even more active role after the adoption of the EU Due Diligence Directive in 2024.

In sum, the current compilation brings together a number of highly original and topical contributions around the general theme of EU participation in multilateral fora. Presenting both the legal challenges and the policy achievements of the EU in various specialised organisations, it is hard to draw some 'general' conclusions. It seems to us that the EU develops gradually in the different fora, depending on its political clout and financial role in the relevant policy field. At the same time, we observe one mega-trend: there is hardly any multilateral forum left in which the EU does not play a (limited) role, which is a clear sign that the EU has become a geo-political actor in its own right, even in an ever less multilateral world.

Frank Hoffmeister and Christine Kaddous
July 2024

CONTENTS

LIST OF CONTRIBUTORS

Andrej Auersperger Matić

Andrej Auersperger Matić is an international legal adviser with over 20 years of experience with advising, litigation, research and teaching of European and international law. Currently he is a Legal Adviser in the Legal Department of the European External Action Service (EEAS) in Brussels, Belgium. His responsibilities include advising on topics such as international courts and justice, the role of the European Union in international organisations, international human rights protection and relations with Central Asia and Africa/MENA, as well as assisting with the negotiation of international agreements. Before joining the EEAS, he was the Legal Adviser to the European Parliament Liaison Office in Washington, DC (2020–22), where he mainly covered transatlantic dialogue on digital tech regulation, and a Member of the European Parliament Legal Service (2005–20). His work in that capacity was principally in the fields of EU institutional law, international agreements (such as TTIP or CETA), trade and investment protection, human rights and civil/criminal law cooperation. He was involved in litigation before the courts of the European Union in 14 cases and in numerous legislative negotiations with the European Commission and the Council of Ministers. Andrej holds a law degree and a master's degree from the University of Ljubljana, an LL.M from Yale Law School and a PhD from Maastricht University. He is the author of *Just Words: The Effectiveness of Civil Justice in European Human Rights Jurisprudence* (Cambridge, Cambridge University Press, 2020).

Michael Braun

Michael Braun is a Junior Professional Officer in the Employment Policy Job Creation and Livelihoods Department at the International Labour Organization in Geneva. He previously worked as an employment lawyer and as a policy officer for the German Federal Ministry of Labour and Social Affairs.

Maurizio Bussi

Maurizio Bussi is the ILO's Director of the Priority Action Programme on Decent Work in Crises and Post-Crisis Situations. He is an international civil servant with more than 25 years of service with the United Nations system who has been involved in complex development and humanitarian operations at the UN and ILO Headquarters in New York and Geneva and served in various field positions, primarily in the Middle East and in Asia. He previously served as Deputy Regional Director for Europe and Central Asia from October 2017 to December 2022 and was the Director of the Bangkok-based ILO Decent Work Technical Support Team for East and South-East Asia and the Pacific (2012–17).

Frank Hoffmeister

Frank Hoffmeister holds a PhD from the University of Heidelberg (1998) and served as academic assistant at the Walter Hallstein-Institute for European Constitutional Law from 1998 until 2001. He then joined the European Commission, where he worked first in the Cyprus Unit in DG Enlargement before becoming a member of the Commission Legal Service (external relations and institutional team). From 2010 to 2014 he acted as Deputy Head of Cabinet for the EU Trade Commissioner De Gucht, and as of 2015 he was Head of Unit dealing with anti-dumping at DG Trade. He joined the European External Action Service in November 2021 as Director for General Affairs and Head of the Legal Department. He teaches international economic law at the Free University of Brussels and has written extensively on EU and international law matters. He edited (together with J Wouters, G Debaere and T Ramopoulos) *The Law of EU External Relations, Cases, Materials and Commentary on the EU as an International Legal Actor*, 3rd edn (Oxford, Oxford University Press, 2021).

Christine Kaddous

Christine Kaddous is Professor of European and International law at the University of Geneva, Jean Monnet Chair *ad personam*. She is also Director of the Centre d'études juridiques européennes (CEJE) and of the Master in European and International Governance (MEIG) Programme. She is Visiting Professor at the Université Paris-Panthéon-Assas and has been Visiting Professor at different universities in France, Belgium and the UK as well as at the College of Europe (Bruges/Natolin). She holds degrees from the University of Neuchâtel, the University of Cambridge and the University Libre de Bruxelles. She practised as a lawyer in the field of Commercial and trade law. She is on the list of chairpersons for arbitrations and TSD expert panel proceedings for dispute settlement under the trade agreements concluded by the EU with third countries. She teaches, researches and consults on international trade law, internal market law, judicial protection, Swiss–EU bilateral agreements and EU external relations law. She has published extensively. Among her recent publications are: 'Switzerland and the EU: The Failure of the Institutional Agreement from a Legal Perspective' (Leiden, Brill,

2023); 'L'impact du principe de coopération loyale sur la politique commerciale de l'Union' (Brussels, Bruylant, 2023); 'Some Thoughts on the EU New Generation of Free Trade Agreements' (Paris, Mare et Martin, 2022); 'L'égalité des États membres dans les relations extérieures de l'Union européenne' (Brussels, Bruylant, 2022).

Christina Kokkinakis

Christina Kokkinakis is Deputy Managing Director Global and Director for Values and Multilateral Relations at the European External Action Service (EEAS). Prior to that she served as Ambassador and Representative of Austria to the Political and Security Committee (PSC) of the European Union. From 2017 until 2019 she worked as Director for the EU Common Foreign and Security Policy (CFSP) at the Austrian Federal Ministry for Europe, Integration and Foreign Affairs. In this function Ms. Kokkinakis was responsible for the EU Foreign Affairs Council (FAC). Before that she worked as Director for the EU Single Market at the Austrian MFA. From 2012 until 2016 she served in the European External Action Service (EEAS) as head of Human rights at the EU Delegation to the United Nations in Geneva. In this capacity, she served as the permanent chair of EU coordination meetings in the field of Human rights in Geneva and she contributed to the EU's policy setting in the field of Human rights at the United Nations in Geneva.

Ms. Kokkinakis joined the Austrian diplomatic service in 1995 and has been active on a range of multilateral (both United Nations and European Union) as well as bilateral issues. From 2009 to 2012, she served as Head of the Political Section at the Permanent Representation of Austria to the EU, responsible for Brussels-based foreign policy working parties. From 2005 to 2009, she was the Deputy Permanent Representative of Austria to the United Nations and other International Organizations in Geneva being responsible for delivering on Austria's contribution to the United Nations in terms of Human rights, humanitarian affairs, health, labour issues, development and disarmament. Prior to that position she served as senior Foreign Policy advisor on UN, the Organization for Security and Cooperation in Europe (OSCE) and the Council of Europe as well as on bilateral relations, with a special focus on the Middle East and Latin America, to two Austrian Foreign Ministers (1998–2001 and 2003–05). Ms. Kokkinakis has had a variety of other responsibilities with the Austrian Federal Ministry for Europe, Integration and Foreign Affairs, including Deputy Head of Mission at the Austrian Embassy in Prague (2001–03). She has furthermore worked in the Department for United Nations as well as in the Austrian Permanent Mission to the United Nations in Vienna and in the Austrian Permanent Mission to the OSCE. From 1996 to 1997 she served as Attachée at the Austrian Cultural Forum in London. Ms. Kokkinakis holds a degree in International Relations (1995), and a Master of Arts degree in History and French literature (1993). Aside from her mother tongue, she is fluent in five languages, English, French, Spanish, Italian and Modern Greek and has some basic knowledge of Dutch.

Flavia Marisi

Dr Flavia Marisi is a Member of the Legal Service of the European Commission, where she represents the European Union in international trade and investment disputes and provides legal advice on matters related to EU and international law. Her experience covers diverse sectors including the environment, energy, climate change, agriculture, food, technology and telecommunications, construction, real estate, and transport. She is a member of the Bar of Pescara (Italy), holds a PhD. from Ghent University, an LL.M. from the College of Europe, Bruges, and an LL.M. from the University of Milan. Prior to joining the European Commission, Dr Marisi practised law in Belgium and Italy, was a researcher at the Chinese University of Hong Kong, and worked at the Court of Justice of the European Union in Luxembourg.

David Mosler

David Mosler is a Technical Officer in the ILO Regional Office for Europe and Central Asia, where he produces applied research on labour market challenges within the region. His recent research has investigated the employment impact of the war in Ukraine, the future of work in the automotive sector, the role of social dialogue in addressing the COVID-19 pandemic, and labour shortages in the Visegrád countries.

Josephine Norris

Josephine Norris is Adjunct Professor at the Vrije Universiteit Brussel, teaching the Law of International Organizations. She has spent the past decade as a Member of the Legal Service at the European Commission advising on European and International law. She is currently in the World Trade Organization (WTO) and international trade law team, and specialises in litigation and arbitration, including WTO dispute settlement. She advises on trade-related aspects of energy and climate change, issues relating to technical barriers to trade and subsidies. Josephine is assistant editor of the *Encyclopaedia of Environmental Law* (Thompson Reuters).

Josephine is a UK-qualified barrister and spent five years in private practice before joining the European Commission. She was appointed to the UK Attorney General's Panel of Counsel.

Josephine studied law at Cambridge University (MA Cantab). She has a Diplôme d'études specialisées – droit européen from the Institute d'études européennes (Université libre de Bruxelles) where she studied as a scholar of the Philippe Wiener – Maurice Anspach Foundation.

Donata Rugarabamu

Donata Rugarabamu is the Legal Counsel of FAO. She has served in a number of intergovernmental organisations, including the Organisation for the Prohibition of Chemical Weapons, the United Nations Environment Programme, the United Nations Compensation Commission and the Commonwealth Secretariat. She has an MA in Law from the University of Cambridge and an LL.M in Public International Law from the London School of Economics and Political Science. She is a Member of the Bar of England and Wales.

Jan Wouters

Jan Wouters is Full Professor of International Law and International Organizations, Jean Monnet Chair *ad personam*, at KU Leuven, Director of the Institute for International Law and of the Leuven Centre for Global Governance Studies (a Jean Monnet and KU Leuven Centre of Excellence), and Administrator of the America Europe Fund at KU Leuven. He is Adjunct Professor at Columbia University (New York) and Visiting Professor at the College of Europe (Bruges) and Université Panthéon-Assas (Paris II). A Member of the Belgian Royal Academy, and *Of Counsel* at Omega Law, he has published widely on international and EU law, international organisations, global governance, corporate and financial law. He recently coordinated two large European projects, FRAME ('Fostering Human Rights Among European External and Internal Policies', 2013–17) and RECONNECT ('Reconnecting Europe with its Citizens through Democracy and Rule of Law', 2018–22). He advises and trains regularly international organisations and governments and is often asked to comment on international events in national and international media.

1

The European Union in International Organisations: Principles and Rules for Good Governance

CHRISTINE KADDOUS

Over the years, the European Community (EC), and at a later stage the European Union (EU), has developed relationships with various international organisations. These relationships have been a logical consequence of the transfer of competences from the Member States to the EC/EU over the past decades. However, not all international organisations accept the EU as a full member, which leads to a variety of arrangements, ranging from situations where the EU has to rely on its Member States to be represented, to situations of EU full membership.

In 2003, the participation of the EU and/or its Member States in international organisations was reaffirmed at the highest level. The European Council considered the concept of 'effective multilateralism' as central to the external action of the EU.[1] At the core of the realisation of this concept was the participation of the EU in the United Nations, but not only that. Its participation in other international fora was also taken into consideration. More recently, in 2021, the European Commission and the High Representative of the Union for Foreign Affairs and Security Policy ('the High Representative') did put forward a strategy to strengthen the EU's contribution to rules-based multilateralism. The idea of the strategy is to serve global governance but to also serve EU global interests and values.[2] Stressing that the EU and its Member States are key participants in the multilateral system,

[1] Revised version of the Presidency Conclusions of the Brussels European Council (12 and 13 December 2003), of 5 February 2004, para 91.

[2] Joint Communication to the European Parliament and the Council on strengthening the EU's contribution to rules-based multilateralism of 17 February 2021 (JOIN (2021) 3 final).

the strategy indicates that they should have a better influence within the system wherever they effectively coordinate their positions, actions and messaging, and act as one, in line with the Treaties.[3]

The increasing participation of the EU in international organisations occurred on the basis of the EU's capacity to exercise rights in international legal transactions and to enter into obligations across the whole field of the Treaties' objectives.[4] The well-established case law on the external competence of the EU played a central role in this evolution.[5] The EU concluded a large number of international agreements with third countries and international organisations. The entry into force of the Lisbon Treaty reinforced this trend. The capacity to participate in international organisations was stressed in Article 21(1) TEU, which provides that the EU seeks 'to develop relations and build partnerships with third countries and international, regional or global organisations'. It is worth noting that whereas the provision distinguishes between two levels of organisations – regional and global – no clear consequences seem to follow from this distinction in practice. According to Article 21(2) TEU, the EU shall work for a high degree of cooperation in all fields of international relations in order to promote an 'international system based on stronger multilateral cooperation and good global governance'.

Given the well-developed case law on the EU's external action and the provisions resulting from the Lisbon Treaty, the EU has become an active member on the international scene, not only as far as international representation is concerned, but also in the conclusion of international agreements and in its participation in multilateral organisations.

The EU is a full member of a great number of international organisations. The best-known ones are the World Trade Organization (WTO) and

[3] Joint Communication to the European Parliament and the Council on strengthening the EU's contribution to rules-based multilateralism of 17 February 2021 (JOIN (2021) 3 final), p 10.

[4] Over the years, the EU's role on the international scene has become the focus of interest of many scholars. See notably E Cannizzaro (ed), *The European Union as an Actor in International Relations* (The Hague, Kluwer Law International, 2002); M Cremona, 'The Union as a Global Actor: Roles, Models and Identity' (2004) 41 *CML Rev* 553–73; P Koutrakos, *EU International Relations Law* (Oxford, Hart Publishing, 2006); C Bretherton and J Vogler, *The European Union as Global Actor* (Routledge, 2006); C Hill and M Smith (eds), *International Relations and the European Union* (Oxford, Oxford University Press, 2011); Bart von Vooren, Steven Blockmans and Jan Wouters (eds), *The EU's role in Global Governance* (Oxford, Oxford University Press, 2013); C Kaddous (ed), *The European Union in International Organisations and Global Governance. Recent Developments* (Oxford, Hart Publishing, 2015); J Czuczai and N Frederik (eds), *The EU as a Global Actor-Bridging Legal Theory and Practice: Liber Amicorum in Honour of Ricardo Gosalbo Bono* (Leiden, Brill, 2017); RA Wessel and J Odermatt (eds), *Research Handbook on the European Union and International Organizations* (Cheltenham, Edward Elgar, 2019).

[5] ECJ, Case 22/70 *Commission v Council* [1971] ECR 263; ECJ, Joined Cases 3/76, 4/76 and 6/76 *Kramer* [1976] ECR 1279; *Opinion 1/76* [1977] ECR 741, and the subsequent case law.

the Food and Agricultural Organization (FAO). Apart from these two famous examples the EU is a member of organisations active in diverse fields, such as Eurocontrol, the European Bank for Reconstruction and Development (EBRD), the Codex Alimentarius Commission (CAC), the Hague Conference on Private International Law, the Intergovernmental Organisation for International Carriage by Rail (OTIF) as well as of regional fisheries organisations.[6] However, the EU is not member of the United Nations (UN) or of any of the major UN organisations (except the FAO). It is not, for example, a member of the International Labour Organization (ILO) or of the International Monetary Fund (IMF) or the World Bank.[7] Therefore, it participates in many international organisations with an observer status, which depends on the text of the constituent charter of the organisation. It benefits, for example, from an observer status at the United Nations Educational, Scientific and Cultural Organization (UNESCO), an enhanced observer status at the General Assembly of the United Nations, and a special position within the Organisation for Economic Cooperation and Development (OECD), which may be considered very close to full membership or de facto membership.[8]

In this global context, one of the issues to be addressed relates to the ways in which the EU participates in international organisations, considering the challenges it has to face internally and externally in terms of governance. In order to answer this question, the present contribution takes into account the practice which has been developed on the basis of the EU Treaties after Lisbon and analyses the principles applicable to EU external representation with its more recent developments (section I), the foundations for the EU's participation in international organisations (section II), as well as the challenges it faces because and following such participation (section III). The concluding section discusses the principles and rules that are applied to ensure a good governance in the area of

[6] Communication from the Commission to the Council and the European Parliament Community – Participation in Regional Fisheries Organisations (RFOs), COM(1999) 613 final. See on that issue, P Heckler, 'Regional Fisheries Organisations. Defining the EU and Member States roles', in *Research Handbook on the European Union and International Organizations* (Cheltenham, Edward Elgar, 2019), 429–45.

[7] C Kaddous, 'European Union Participation in International Financial Organizations', in I Govaere and S Poli (eds), *EU Management of Global Emergencies*, Studies in EU External Relations (Leiden, Brill 2014), 277–95; P Leino, 'On the Duty of Cooperation, Consistency and Influence in the External Relations of the Euro-Zone: Representation of EU and EU Member States in the International Monetary Fund', in *European Yearbook of International Economic Law 2017* (Springer 2017), 563–96; E Castellarin, The EU's participation in the global financial world, in *Research Handbook on the European Union and International Organizations* (Cheltenham, Edward Elgar, 2019), 293–315.

[8] See notably F Vlastou-Dimopoulou, 'Organisation for Economic Co-operation and Development (OECD), The EU's position as a de facto Member', in RA Wessel (ed), *Research Handbook on the European Union and International Organizations* (Cheltenham, Edward Elgar, 2019, 316–37.

the participation of the EU and its Member States in international organisations (section IV).

I. Principles and Rules Applicable to EU External Representation

The issue of external representation dates back to the historical judgment of 1964 in the *Costa v ENEL* case. Referring to the creation of the European Economic Community, to its institutions and to its own personality, the Court of justice recognised the Community's capacity of representation on the international scene.[9] This capacity of external representation is reflected today in the exercise of the 'right of legation'[10] and in the ability of the EU to participate in international organisations with the status of observer or full member.

Today, the EU's external representation lies within the recognition of its legal personality, which is today enshrined in Article 47 TEU. Before Lisbon, the situation was different. The EC had legal personality *explicitly* conferred by Article 281 TEC, while the EU had 'only' de facto legal personality, resulting from the practice that developed in relation to the previous Articles 24 and 38 TEU. An illustration of this practice was given by the conclusion of EU agreements with the US in the fields of extradition and legal assistance in 2003,[11] and with Switzerland for its association to Schengen in 2004.[12] This practice did not raise any objection from the EU Member States, nor from third countries.

After the explicit recognition of the EU's legal personality in the Lisbon Treaty, the participation of the EU in international organisations increased. The merging of the EU and the EC into one single entity was a facilitator. It allowed a better identification of the EU, as a single actor, on the international scene. It also had the advantage of putting an end to the confusion related to the coexistence of the EU and the EC and their respective competences in the field of external

[9] ECJ, Case 6/64, *Costa v ENEL* [1964] ECR 1141, 1159.

[10] The right of legation is the right of the European Union to receive diplomatic missions from third States. It also covers the right to have diplomatic missions in third states. The EU is represented today through some 144 EU delegations and offices around the world.

[11] Agreement on extradition between the European Union and the United States of America, OJ L 181, 19.7.2003, p 27; Agreement on mutual legal assistance between the European Union and the United States of America, OJ L 181, 19.7.2003, p 34.

[12] Agreement between the European Union, the European Community and the Swiss Confederation on the Swiss Confederation's association with the implementation, application and development of the Schengen acquis, OJ L 53, 27.2.2008, p 52.

action. The merging of the EC and the EU increased legibility and clarity in the relations with third countries and international organisations, which have today as their partner one general representative: the EU – if one leaves aside the Euratom Community which provides competences linked to the atomic energy field.[13] However, one should not underestimate the fact that, despite the improvement brought about by the 'single partner', the EU is composed of Member States that may also be parties, along with the EU, to international organisations. The joint participation of the EU and its Member States raises complex issues as to the division of competences[14] and as to EU representation.

As a matter of fact, the EU is sometimes participating alone in the international organisation, sometimes together with its Member States, and sometimes the EU does not participate as such but only the Member States are parties to the international organisation. These different scenarios depend on legal and political factors, among which the issues of the division of competences between the EU and its Member States and whether or not the EU can participate as such in the organisation as a 'regional economic international organisation' (REIO).[15]

As to the EU's external representation, the Treaties provide for some rules. In matters other than the Common Foreign and Security Policy (CFSP), the representation is entrusted to the European Commission, the rotating Presidency, the EU delegations and the Member States based on the division of competences between the EU and its Member States. In principle, where the competence is exclusive, the European Commission represents the Union. Where the competence is shared, the rotating Presidency and the European Commission participate in the representation of the Union, subject to the more concrete following developments.

In CFSP matters, the representation of the EU is shared between the President of the European Council, the High Representative, the EU delegations and the Member States.[16] Article 15(6) TEU provides that the President of the European Council shall, at his or her level and in that capacity, ensure the external representation of the EU on issues concerning CFSP, without prejudice to the powers of the High Representative. In parallel, Article 27(2) TEU provides that the High

[13] The European Atomic Energy Community survived the entry into force of the Lisbon Treaty.

[14] See section III.

[15] See my observations below, under section II.

[16] On the High Representative, see notably C Kaddous, 'Role and Position of the High Representative of the Union for Foreign Affairs and Security Policy under the Lisbon Treaty', in S Griller and J Ziller (eds), *The Lisbon Treaty. Eu Constitutionalism without a Constitution Treaty?* (Vienna/New York, Springer Verlag, 2008), 205–23.

Representative shall represent the Union in matters relating to the CFSP, shall conduct political dialogue with third parties on the Union's behalf and shall express the 'Union's position in international organisations', all with the assistance of the EEAS. The role of the Member States in CFSP matters is dealt with in Declaration 13, which recalls that the adoption of the provisions in the TFEU covering this policy, including the creation of the office of High Representative and the establishment of the EEAS, does not affect the responsibilities of the Member States, as they existed, for the formulation and conduct of their foreign policy nor their national representation in third countries and international organisations.[17]

According to Article 221(1) TFEU, Union delegations in third countries and at international organisations shall represent the Union. These delegations are placed under the overall authority of the High Representative (Article 221(2) TFEU). On that basis, the High Representative has the power to instruct Union delegations about what to say and when.[18] This is true insofar as the topics relate to CFSP. The Union delegations mirror the power of the High Representative to represent the Union externally in CFSP matters.

In matters other than CFSP, Union delegations are also entitled under Article 221(1) TFEU to represent the EU. However, their instructions will not come from the High Representative, but rather from the relevant Commissioners and their services in the headquarters in Brussels in their respective areas of competence.[19]

The situation is more complex when it comes to statements that touch not only upon EU matters but also national matters, the so-called 'mixed' situations. This gave raise to divergences of interpretation with regard to the division of competences between the EU and its Member States. In 2011 after the adoption by the UN General Assembly of the Resolution on the participation of the EU in the work of the organisation with an enhanced observer status,[20] the UK, still an EU Member State at that time, blocked several statements that had to be delivered by the EU within the UN.[21] The reason was a disagreement as to

[17] Declaration 13 annexed to the final act of the intergovernmental conference which adopted the Treaty of Lisbon, signed on 13 December 2007.

[18] See in this regard F Hoffmeister, 'Of Presidents, High Representatives and European Commissioners: the External Representation of the European Union Seven Years after Lisbon', in (2017) *Europe and the World: A Law Review* 1, 15–17.

[19] Article 5(3) of Council Decision 2010/427/EU establishing the organisation and functioning of the European External Action Service, OJ L 201 3.8.2010, p 30.

[20] Resolution A/65/PV.88 of 3 May 2011, UN Doc A/RES/65/276.

[21] J Borger, 'EU Anger over British stance on UN Statements', *The Guardian*, 20 October 2011, states: 'The other 26 member states objected, arguing that the UK was using a technicality to stop the EU

who should deliver the statements. The UK Delegation to the UN considered that these statements were to be made by representatives of the EU 'on behalf of the European Union and its Member States' and not on behalf of the EU alone. This divergence created a true crisis in EU external representation. A solution has been found which is enshrined in the 'EU Statements in multilateral organisations. General Arrangements' adopted by the Council of the European Union in October 2011.[22] This document recalls that the Lisbon Treaty enables the EU to achieve coherent, comprehensive and unified external representation. It refers to the close and sincere cooperation provided for in the Treaties between the Member States and the EU and incorporates the principles laid down in the relevant case law of the Court of Justice. The document stresses that the preparation of statements relating to the sensitive area of competences of the EU and its Member States should 'remain internal and consensual', introducing thereby a kind of disconnection between what happens internally within the EU and what is expressed externally at the international level.[23]

As a result of these Arrangements the EU can only make a statement in the cases where it is competent and where there is a position which has been agreed upon in accordance with the relevant Treaty provisions.[24] The Member States and the EU actors – defined in the document as being the President of the European Council, the Commission, the High Representative and EU Delegations – have to coordinate their action in international organisations to the fullest extent possible, as set out in the Treaties. More concretely, positions common to the EU and its Member States should be made 'on behalf of the EU and its Member States', whereas if the Member States agree to collective representation by an EU actor of issues relating to the exercise of national competences, the statement will be prefaced by 'on behalf of the Member States'.[25] It is also possible that the Member States agree on a case-by-case basis whether and how to coordinate and be represented externally.[26] The Member States may request EU actors or a Member State, notably the Member State holding the rotating Presidency of the Council, to do so on their behalf.

mission from functioning properly and to prevent the EU from speaking in one voice on important issues even when all the members were in full agreement', see http://www.theguardian.com/world/2011/oct/20/uk-eu-un-statements-wording.

[22] Council of the European Union, *EU Statements in Multilateral Organisations. General Arrangements*, Document 16901/11, 24 October 2011.

[23] ibid, point 2.

[24] ibid, point 3.

[25] ibid, point 4, 2nd bullet.

[26] ibid, point 3, 5th bullet.

Consequently, unity of representation is guaranteed to the extent that the Member States seek to ensure and promote possibilities for the EU actors to deliver statements on behalf of the EU. The Member States may complement statements made on behalf of the EU whilst respecting the principle of sincere cooperation.[27]

These Arrangements are intended to be applied broadly unless more specific practical arrangements, such as those at the WTO or at the FAO exist for coordination and/or representation.[28] Despite the fact that they do not deal with the core and sensitive issue of the division of competences, which should be determined internally and consensually, the Arrangements bring helpful and concrete rules on EU external representation and allow the determination of 'who' is going to represent 'the EU', once the internal question of competences is agreed upon. In that sense, the document presents the advantage of regulating the daily business life of the EU and its Member States within international organisations. This is progress, even if the expectations were higher.[29]

The EU's participation in the WTO gives a completely different picture from the one described above in the UN Family. First, the Arrangements of 2011 do not apply to the WTO. Second, the EU is full member of the organisation along with its Member States. According to Article 17(1) TEU, the European Commission represents the EU in the area of trade. At the level of Heads of State this role falls to the Commission President and at the level of Ministers, to the EU Trade Commissioner. The EU ambassador accredited to the WTO is (like all EU ambassadors) an official of the EEAS, but receives instructions from the Commission headquarters. It is only where a WTO matter is covered not by an EU competence but by a national competence that the situation would be different, as it is for budgetary discussions.[30] In such instances, Member States may choose whether they wish to express themselves individually or entrust the Presidency of the Council to speak on their behalf.

[27] This last duty led some commentators, J Larik and A Delgado Casteleiro, to write an article entitled 'The duty to remain Silent: Limitless Loyalty in EU External Relations' (2011) 35(4) *European Law Review* 524–41. On the principle of sincere cooperation, see the collective book with many contributions on the principle in different fields of EU external action: M Fartunova-Michel and JF Delile (eds), *La coopération loyale dans le droit des relations extérieures de l'Union européenne. Collection Droit de l'Union européenne. Colloques* (Brussels, Bruylant, 2023).

[28] *General Arrangements*, n 22 above, point 3.

[29] In the same sense, see RA Wessel and J Larik (eds), *EU External Relations Law, Text, cases and Materials* (Cambridge, Cambridge University Press, 2020), 560.

[30] Each Member State contributes to the lump sum payable by the EU as its contribution to the WTO. On the participation of the Union within the WTO, see Josephine Norris and Flavia Marisi, Chapter 2 in this volume; see also J Wouters, F Hoffmeister, G De Baere and T Ramopoulos, *The Law of EU External Relations. Cases, Materials and Commentary on the EU as an International Legal Actor* (Oxford, Oxford University Press, 2021), 559.

As a result of the foregoing the external representation of the EU is governed by the Treaties provisions, by the 2011 Arrangements as well as by more specific rules like the ones applicable at the WTO or at the FAO. In addition, the principles of unity and of sincere cooperation play an important role in EU external representation. As stated in the case law,[31] the sincere cooperation principle is of general application in the external actions of the EU and does not depend on the nature of the competences of the EU, whether exclusive or shared.[32] At the same time, as will be examined below, the division of competences between the EU and its Member States is fundamental to the participation of the EU in international organisations.

II. The Foundations for EU Participation in International Organisations

The foundations of EU participation in international organisations are dual. They relate first to the division of competences between the EU and its Member States (subsection II.A), and second to the statute of the international organisation in question and the various possible forms of EU participation (subsection II.B).

A. Division of Competences between the EU and its Member States

According to Article 216 TFEU, the EU is empowered to conclude international agreements with third countries or international organisations. In addition, Articles 220 and 221 TFEU relate to the Union's relations with international organisations, third countries and EU delegations.[33]

[31] ECJ, Case C-266/03, *Commission v Luxembourg* [2005] ECR I-4805, para 58; Case C-433/03, *Commission v Germany* [2005] ECR I-6985, para 64; Case C-246/07, *Commission v Sweden* (PFOS) [2010] ECR I-3317, para 71.

[32] On the application of the principle of sincere cooperation in the field of CCP, see C Kaddous, 'L'impact du principe de coopération loyale sur la politique commerciale de l'Union', in M Farturova-Michel and JF Delile (eds), *La coopération loyale dans le droit des relations extérieures de l'Union européenne. Collection Droit de l'Union européenne. Colloques* (Brussels, Bruylant, 2023), 193–212.

[33] F Hoffmeister, 'Ousider or Frontrunner? Recent Developments under International and European Law on the Status of the European Union in International Organisations and Treaty Bodies' (2007) 44 *CML Rev* 41; C Kaddous (ed), *The European Union in International Organisations and Global Governance. Recent Developments* (Oxford, Hart Publishing, 2015); J Czuczai and N Frederik (eds), *The EU as a Global Actor-Bridging Legal Theory and Practice: Liber Amicorum in Honour of Ricardo Gosalbo Bono* (Leiden, Brill, 2017); RA Wessel and J Odermatt (eds), *Research Handbook on the European Union and International Organizations* (Cheltenham, Edward Elgar, 2019).

By virtue of Article 220 TFEU, the Union

> shall establish all appropriate forms of cooperation with the organs of the United Nations and its specialised agencies, the Council of Europe, the Organisation for Security and Co-operation in Europe [OSCE] and the Organisation for Economic Cooperation and Development [OECD].

It must also maintain such relations as are appropriate with other international organisations. The High Representative and the Commission shall implement this provision. On the other hand, Article 221 provides that 'Union delegations in third countries and at international organisations shall represent the Union'. These are placed under the authority of the High Representative and they act in close cooperation with Member States' diplomatic and consular missions. Furthermore, other provisions of the TFEU deal with cooperation at the international level with respect to specific fields, such as education and sport (Article 165 TFEU), vocational training (Article 166 TFEU), culture (Article 167 TFEU), public health (Article 168 TFEU), research and technological development (Article 180 TFEU), space (Article 189 TFEU), environment (Article 191 TFEU), common commercial policy (Article 207 TFEU), development cooperation (Article 209 TFEU), economic, financial and technical cooperation (Article 212 TFEU), humanitarian aid (Article 214 TFEU) and monetary or foreign exchange (Article 219 TFEU).

All these provisions do not expressly provide for EU membership of international organisations but for cooperation with such organisations. It is through case law that the EU's capacity to participate as such in international organisations has been recognised. In the ECJ's *Opinion 1/76*, it was considered that the Community was not only entitled to enter into contractual relations with a third country but also had the power, while observing the provisions of the Treaty, to cooperate with that country in setting up an appropriate organism such as the public international institution which was proposed to be established in the case at issue.[34] This principle of participation was later implicitly confirmed in *Opinion 1/94*[35] where the Court recognised the competence of the European Communities to create the WTO with the other members of the organisation.

[34] ECJ, *Opinion 1/76*, Draft Agreement establishing a European Laying-up fund for inland waterway vessels, [1977] ECR 741, para 5.

[35] ECJ, *Opinion 1/94*, Competence of the Community to conclude the WTO agreements [1994] ECR I-5267.

Once the basic principle of Union participation in international organisations was established, the debates focused on the division of competences between the EU and its Member States in order to determine 'who' among them will be empowered to participate in a specific international organisation. According to the Treaties and to case-law, the EU participates alone in an international organisation where it enjoys exclusive competence. It participates jointly with the Member States where the competence is not exclusive.

In cases of EU non-exclusive competence, and regarding the relationship between the EU on one hand and the Member States on the other hand, the duty of sincere cooperation plays a central role. The Court of justice had the opportunity in *Opinions 2/91*[36] and *1/94*,[37] to assert that this duty of cooperation between the European institutions and the Member States results from the requirement of unity in the international representation of the Community – today of the EU. It applies both in the process of negotiation and conclusion of an international agreement or convention as well as in the fulfilment of the obligations entered into thereunder.

However, the EU's participation in international organisations also depends on one element which is not a matter of EU law. The constituent treaty of the organisation in question should allow membership for REIOs. Otherwise only the EU Member States will be able to take part in the said organisation. In other words, the constituent treaty of the international organisation determines whether the EU can participate, and if so, in what form.

[36] ECJ, *Opinion 2/91*, Convention N° 170 of the International Labour Organization concerning safety in the use of chemicals at work, [1993] ECR I-1061, para 36: '... when it appears that the subject-matter of an agreement or contract falls in part within the competence of the Community and in part within that of the Member States, it is important to ensure that there is a close association between the institutions of the Community and the Member States both in the process of negotiation and conclusion and in the fulfilment of the obligations entered into. This duty of cooperation, to which attention was drawn in the context of the EAEC Treaty, must also apply in the context of the EEC Treaty since it results from the requirement of unity in the international representation of the Community.'

[37] ECJ, *Opinion 1/94*, Competence of the Community to conclude the WTO agreements, [1994] ECR I-5267, para 108: 'where it is apparent that the subject-matter of an agreement or convention falls in part within the competence of the Community and in part within that of the Member States, it is essential to ensure close cooperation between the Member States and the Community institutions, both in the process of negotiation and conclusion and in the fulfilment of the commitments entered into. That obligation to cooperate flows from the requirement of unity in the international representation of the Community.' See notably C Kaddous, 'L'impact du principe de coopération loyale sur la politique commerciale de l'Union', in M Fartunova and JF Delile (eds), *La coopération loyale dans le droit des relations extérieures de l'Union européenne. Colloques* (Brussels, Bruylant, 2023).

B. Forms of EU Participation in International Organisations

The participation of the EU in international organisations may take different forms, varying from the status of observer (i) to that of full membership (ii). In addition, there is more than one type of observer status, the differences depending on the constituent treaty of the organisation, which may in some cases allow for more active participation by the EU and consequently greatly reduce the differences between members and non-members.[38]

(i) Observer Status

When the EU has very limited powers in the field of the organisation's activities, or when the statute establishing the relevant international organisation does not allow full membership and/or the EU Member States oppose this latter status, the Union may nevertheless be eligible for observer status.

The rights and obligations of the observer are determined in each case by reference to the constituent charter of the organisation. Usually, observers enjoy the right of access to meetings, the right to speak, the right to take part in the discussions and the right to obtain official documentation. Nevertheless, the status of observer does not give the right to vote.

The EU is not a member of the United Nations or of any of the major UN organisations, except the FAO. It has held, as mentioned above, 'enhanced observer' status at the UN General Assembly since 2011.[39] The participation rights of the EU at the UN allow its representatives to present the EU's agreed common positions, to make interventions, present proposals and circulate EU communications as official documents.[40] Whereas all EU Member States participate in the UN General Assembly, only a few of them participate in the Security Council. The EU as such is not represented in this organ. However, Article 34(2) TEU empowers the EU Member States which are also members of the UN Security Council to 'concert and keep the other EU Member States and

[38] See F Hoffmeister, 'Outsider or Frontrunner? Recent developments under International and European Law on the Status of the European Union in International Organisations and treaty bodies' (2007) 44 *CML Rev* 41.

[39] A/RES/65/276, Resolution adopted by the General Assembly on 3 May 2011, *Participation of the European Union in the work of the United Nations.*

[40] On the role of the European Union in the UN, and in particular at the UN Human Rights Council, see the contribution of Christina Kokkinakis and Andrej Auersperger Matić, Chapter 7 in this volume.

the High Representative fully informed'. They are required, in the execution of their functions, to defend the positions and the interests of the EU, without prejudice to their responsibilities under the provisions of the UN Charter. The same provision also provides that when the EU has defined a position on a subject which is on the UN Security Council agenda, those Member States which sit on the Security Council shall request that the High Representative be invited to present the EU's position.

To take another example, the ILO presents the particularity that the EU, although it does have competences in the field of social policy, is not a member of the organisation, because the ILO constitution does not allow for EU membership.[41] The complex division of competences between the EU and its Member States in the ILO was notably addressed in *Opinion 2/91*.[42] The EU also has observer status at the WHO[43] as well as at WIPO.[44]

On the other hand, EU claims to full membership status in international organisations have faced many obstacles.

(ii) Full Membership

The status of full participation of the EU in international organisations has raised difficulties, the most important of which are institutional and political. At the institutional level, the fact that the constituent charters of international organisations generally reserve membership status to states alone implies that the participation of the EU cannot be achieved without a modification of these acts. The more political obstacle, still present today, lies in the fact that Member States of the EU are not necessarily in favour of abandoning their role in international fora and allowing the EU to take over their rights and powers. The EU Member States are often prepared to accept that the EU joins the 'club' but not that it replaces them.

If the constituent charter of the organisation allows the EU to be a member and if its participation is joint with the Member States, the situation becomes

[41] On the participation of the European Union in the ILO, see the contributions of Maurizio Bussi, Michael Braun and David Mosler (Chapter 4) as well as of Frank Hoffmeister, Chapter 5 in this volume.

[42] ECJ, *Opinion 2/91*, Convention N° 170 of the International Labour Organisation concerning safety in the use of chemicals at work, [1993] ECR I-1061.

[43] On the conditions of this participation as well as the evaluation of the role of the Union in the WHO, see the contribution of Frank Hoffmeister, Chapter 5 in this volume.

[44] On the participation of the European Union in WIPO, see the contribution of J-C Galloux, 'The European Union in the World Intellectual Property Organization: From a Cloudy Complexity towards an Ordered Pluralism: An External Appraisal', in C Kaddous (ed), *The European Union in International Organisations and Global Governance: Recent Developments* (Oxford, Hart Publishing, 2015), 223.

complex both within the EU and within the international organisation itself, in particular with regard to the issue of which of the EU or the Member States may exercise the rights attached to membership.[45]

It is not only the EU Member States which are opposed to the granting of membership to the EU in international organisations. Third states have in the past invoked the legally imprecise nature of the EU and the issues related to its international responsibility. In particular, they have (wrongly) questioned the EU's ability to compel its Member States to respect the commitments made by it at the international level.[46] They have also highlighted the danger of setting precedents, the risk of encouraging the formation of blocs within the organisation by the accession of the EU (making the decision more difficult), and the problems related to the simultaneous membership of the EU and its Member States in the same international organisation. This resistance by third states is still present today.

Despite these internal and external objections, the EU was granted the status of full membership in many organisations,[47] the most famous example being the WTO. The status of full membership puts the EU on an equal footing with the Member States of the organisation. The EU thus acquires the right to vote, the right to make proposals and the right to speak.

The difficulties raised by the EU's participation lie in the fact that, most often, it is not involved alone in the organisation, but alongside its Member States. This joint participation is explained by the division of competences between the EU and its Member States. Very often, there is a 'mixity' situation, based on the fact that many competences are shared between the EU and its Member States.

Joint membership of the EU and its Member States raises a number of important issues, particularly in relation to the decision-making process and

[45] For an illustration of this difficulty, see ECJ, Case C-25/94, *Commission v Council*, [1996] ECR I-1469 and my observations below under section III.

[46] The existence of the infringement procedure of Articles 258–260 TFEU proves that this is not true. Furthermore, the case law has demonstrated that the Commission does not hesitate to bring the matter before the ECJ when it considers that a Member State has failed to comply with commitments made by the EU on the international scene. ECJ, Case C-61/94, *Commission v Germany*, [1996] ECR I-3989, para 41 or ECJ, Case C-45/07, *Commission v Greece*, [2007] ECR I-4185.

[47] To be precise, one may indeed distinguish two kinds of participation as a member. The first gives the possibility to the European Union to accede an international organisation, as such, an organisation that has an independent existence with a developed structure. The second type occurs in the case of an international agreement on a specific subject, creating a kind of organisational structure between the parties, in order to implement its provisions.

voting rights. How many votes are provided for the EU in the internal rules of the organisation? How will, and can, these rights be exercised? Two possible models may be envisaged. The voting rights may be exercised alternatively by the EU or by its Member States, or these rights may be cumulated, allowing the EU to add its own vote to those of the Member States. The cumulative vote is opposed by the other members of the organisation, considering this modality as an expression of a new kind of over-representation of the EU and its Member States within the organisation. The alternative way of exercising voting rights requires a definition of the specific cases in which the EU votes and those in which the Member States vote, based presumably on a clear delineation of the powers between the EU and the Member States in the fields of the organisation's activities.

In 1995 the European Communities became founding members, along with their Member States, of the WTO. At the time of membership negotiations, one of the problems that had to be solved was how to regulate the voting rights within the WTO, because the Communities could have been perceived by third states as additional members of the organisation. The solution was the alternative vote.[48] Today, when the EU votes, it gets the number of votes equal to the number of its Member States that are members of the WTO. It must nevertheless be stressed that the voting rules apply as an exception only within the WTO, due to the fact that decisions are generally taken through consensus by the members.

Since the entry into force of the Lisbon Treaty, common commercial policy falls within the exclusive competence of the EU and covers not only trade in goods, but also trade in services, trade-related intellectual property rights and foreign direct investment. As a consequence of this exclusivity, the European Commission enjoys the responsibility for conducting trade negotiations and for representing the EU in international fora. The Member States seem to have accepted the leading role of the EU in the WTO, even if new issues on the negotiator position of the Commission arise between the protagonists.[49]

In the international organisations to which the EU participates as a full member or as an observer, along with the Member States, the issue of coordination is fundamental and constitutes one of the main challenges the EU has to face.

[48] Article IX of the WTO Agreement.

[49] On the participation of the Union within the WTO, see the contribution of Josephine Norris and Flavia Marisi, Chapter 2 in this volume, as well as the contributions of D Brauns, T Baert, J Volkai and F Hoffmeister, in C Kaddous (ed), *The European Union in International Organisations and Global Governance. Recent Developments* (Oxford, Hart Publishing, 2015), respectively 109 and 121.

III. Challenges Linked to EU Participation in International Organisations

The challenges are different depending on the ways in which the EU participates in an international organisation. If the EU may become a full member alongside its Member States, this implies the existence of a shared competence which results in a joint participation of the EU and the Member States in the same international organisation. However, very often the EU does have competences in the field of activity of the international organisation, but the constituent charter of the said organisation does not allow for EU membership. In this precise situation, only the Member States participate in the international organisation – in principle all of them or, depending on the organisation, only some of them.[50] In addition, in these two last scenarios the EU may or may not have observer status.

In the present contribution, the focus will be on two main challenges. The first relates to the coordination between the EU and the Member States (subsection III.A) and the second deals with the establishment of positions to be adopted by the EU in an international organisation (subsection III.B).

A. Coordination between the EU and its Member States in International Organisations

The issue of coordination in the field of external relations arose quite early in the case law of the Court of Justice. In *Opinion 1/78*, it was pointed out that when it appears that the subject-matter of an agreement or a contract falls under the category of shared competences, it is important to ensure that close cooperation between the institutions and the Member States takes place both in the process of negotiation and conclusion of the agreement and in the fulfilment of the obligations entered into. That obligation to cooperate flows from the requirement of unity in international representation.[51]

In the subsequent case law, in *Opinions 2/91*[52] and *1/94*,[53] the duty of close cooperation between the Member States and the Community institutions was

[50] For example, the OIV, see ECJ, Case C-399/12, *Germany v Council* (OIV), EU:C:2014:2258.
[51] ECJ, *Opinion 1/78*, [1978] ECR 2151, paras 34–36.
[52] ECJ, *Opinion 2/91*, Convention N° 170 of the International Labour Organization concerning safety in the use of chemicals at work, [1993] ECR I-1061, para 36.
[53] ECJ, *Opinion 1/94*, Competence of the Community to conclude the WTO agreements, [1994] ECR I-5267, para 108.

examined in relation to participation in the ILO and in the WTO, which present different legal situations. In the ILO, only the Member States participate in the international organisation, whereas the European Communities, and then the European Union, became contracting parties of the WTO, along with the Member States. It follows from the case law that the principle of cooperation applies whether the EU is member of the international organisation or not. From that point, two lines of case law have been developed: the first concerning situations where the EU and its Member States participate in the international organisation: the WTO (*Opinion 1/94*) and FAO (*Commission v Council*[54]) cases; the second covering situations where only the Member States are members of the international organisation or parties to the international agreement: the ILO (*Opinion 2/91*), IMO (*Commission v Greece*[55]) and PFOS (*Commission v Sweden*[56]) cases. These two lines of case law are examined below.

In the 1996 *Commission v Council* case, the Court of justice had to deal with the joint participation of the EU and the Member States in the FAO. The main issue at stake related to the internal Arrangement between the Council and the Commission on the right to vote in said organisation.[57] The two institutions had concluded an internal Arrangement for the preparation of FAO meetings, interventions and voting rights. *In casu*, the Commission brought an action for annulment of the decision of the Council giving the Member States the right to vote in the FAO on the adoption of an agreement to promote compliance with conservation and management measures by fishing vessels on the high seas.

Pursuant to the FAO Constitution, the European Community made a declaration, at the time of its acceptance into the international organisation (1991), specifying that it had exclusive competence in, inter alia, all matters concerning fisheries aimed at protecting fishing grounds and conserving the biological resources of the sea.[58] As regards the rights attaching to membership, the General Rules of the FAO provide for a system of alternative exercise as between the Member Organization and its own Member States, as follows:

> Before any meeting of the Organization the Member Organization or its Member States shall indicate which, as between the Member Organization and its Member States,

[54] ECJ, Case C-25/94, *Commission v Council* [1996] ECR I-1469.

[55] ECJ, Case C-45/07, *Commission v Greece* [2009] ECR I-701, concerning membership of the International Maritime Organization (IMO).

[56] ECJ, Case C-246/07, *Commission v Sweden* [2010] ECR I-3317. The case relates to the Stockholm Convention on Persistent Organic Pollutants and banning the use of perfluoroctane sulfonic acid (PFOS).

[57] ECJ, Case C-25/94, *Commission v Council* [1996] ECR I-1469.

[58] ECJ, Case C-25/94, *Commission v Council* [1996] ECR I-1469, para 3.

has competence … and which, as between the Member Organization and its Member States, shall exercise the right to vote in respect of each particular agenda item.

In cases where an agenda item covers both matters in respect of which competence has been transferred to the Member Organization and matters which lie within the competence of its Member States, both the Member Organization and its Member States may participate in the discussions. In such cases the meeting, in arriving at its decisions, shall take into account only the intervention of the party which has the right to vote.[59]

In the case of the adoption of the agreement within the FAO, the Commission proposed to the Council that the 'shared competence formula' provided for in the internal Arrangement concluded in 1991 between the Commission and the Council should apply.[60] It nonetheless proposed a vote by the European Community, since the thrust of the agreement fell within the area of conservation of fishery resources, for which the Community had competence. Whilst the Commission and the Member States acknowledged that this was a matter for shared competence, they disagreed over the question of the right to vote.

[59] ECJ, Case C-25/94, *Commission v Council* [1996] ECR I-1469, para 4.
[60] ECJ, Case C-25/94, *Commission v Council* [1996] ECR I-1469, paras 6 and 7.

'The Arrangement sets up a coordination procedure to decide on the exercise of responsibilities or on statements on a particular point. Sections 1.12 and 1.13 of the Arrangement provide:

"*1.12* In the absence of an agreement between the Commission and the Member States … , the matter will be decided according to the procedure provided for in the Treaty and the agreed practice. In the absence of agreement on this basis, the matter will be referred to the Permanent Representatives Committee [Coreper].

1.13 Decisions referred to in 1.12 are without prejudice to the respective competences of the Community and its Member States."

The relevant provisions of the rules on statements and voting in FAO meetings are in Section 2. Section 2.1 to 2.3 stipulates as follows:

"*2.1* Where an agenda item deals with matters of exclusive Community competence, the Commission shall speak and vote for the Community.

2.2 Where an agenda item deals with matters of national competence, Member States shall speak and vote.

2.3 Where an agenda item deals with matters containing elements both of national and of Community competence, the aim will be to achieve a common position by consensus. If a common position can be achieved:

— the Presidency shall express the common position when the thrust of the issue lies in an area outside the exclusive competence of the Community. Member States and the Commission may speak to support and/or to add to the Presidency statement. Member States will vote in accordance with the common position;
— the Commission shall express the common position when the thrust of the issue lies in an area within the exclusive competence of the Community. Member States may speak to support and/or add to the Commission's statement. The Commission will vote in accordance with the common position."'

Thus, on the one hand, the Commission proposed to the Member States the adoption of a draft agreement prepared within the FAO. On the other hand, the Council confirmed an earlier decision of the COREPER, under which it was not the Commission but the Member States who should vote in the FAO Conference concerning the adoption of the envisaged agreement. After a thorough examination, the Court of justice held that the Council had violated one of the aspects of the international Arrangement and therefore its decision had to be annulled.

Clearly, joint participation in an international organisation requires coordination between the EU and its Member States and respect of the principle of sincere cooperation enshrined in Article 4(3) TEU. According to this provision, the EU and the Member States shall, in full mutual respect, assist each other in carrying out tasks which flow from the Treaties.[61] This principle shall also prevent the Member States from taking any measure which could jeopardise the attainment of EU's objectives.

The other line of case law has been well illustrated in the IMO and the PFOS cases, rendered respectively in 2009 and 2010, which cover the situation where only the Member States are allowed to participate in the international organisation or international conference.[62]

In *Commission v Greece*, the main issue was to determine whether Greece, a member of the International Maritime Organization (IMO), was entitled to submit a proposal to the IMO, on its own behalf, in an area covered by EU law.[63] The European Commission argued that the EU had enjoyed exclusive competence to assume international obligations in the area covered by the relevant Regulation since its adoption, as the Regulation operated to integrate into EU law provisions of the SOLAS Convention and the ISPS Code.[64] For the Commission, the EU alone was competent to ensure that the standards on the subject were properly applied at EU level and to discuss with other IMO contracting parties the correct implementation of subsequent developments in those standards. Therefore, in the Commission's opinion, the Member States no longer had competence to submit to the IMO national positions on matters falling within the exclusive competence

[61] Article 4 (3) also provides that: 'The Member States shall take any appropriate measure, general or particular, to ensure fulfilment of the obligations arising out of the treaties or resulting from the acts of the institutions of the Union. The Member States shall facilitate the achievement of the Union's tasks and refrain from any measure which could jeopardise the attainment of the Union's objectives'.

[62] ECJ, Case C-45/07, *Commission v Greece* (IMO) [2009] ECR I-701; ECJ, Case C-246/07 *Commission v Sweden* (PFOS) [2010] ECR I-3317.

[63] ECJ, Case C-45/07, *Commission v Greece* (IMO) [2009] ECR I-701.

[64] The Convention for the Safety of Life at Sea (SOLAS Convention) and the International Ship and Port Facility Security Code (ISPS Code).

of the EU, unless expressly authorised to do so by the EU.[65] Given these elements, the Commission alleged a violation by Greece of Article 4(3) TEU as well as of the provisions of the Treaty on common transport policy, in formulating a proposal within the IMO which might have affected the Regulation in the meaning of the judgment in *Commission v Council* (AETR).[66]

Following the Commission, the Court held that Greece had taken an initiative which could have led to the adoption by the IMO of rules likely to affect the provisions of that Regulation. In those circumstances, such behaviour had to be regarded as constituting an infringement of the obligations under Article 4(3) as well as under the provisions of the Treaty on common transport policy.[67]

It follows from the case law that the duty of cooperation entails many commitments; it may require positive actions from the Member States, but also abstentions in order to achieve the Treaties' objectives. The sincere cooperation duty appears to govern not only the situation where both the EU and its Member States participate in the international organisation, but also that where only the Member States are members of the organisation, provided that the organisation is active in areas which fall under the EU's competence. It does not matter whether the competence is exclusive (eg the IMO case) or shared (eg the PFOS case).[68] This duty is to be respected in the whole field of the external action.[69]

Therefore, coordination between the EU and its Member States as well as respect for sincere cooperation, are fundamental rules and principles to ensure effective representation and participation of the EU in international organisations, whether or not the EU is a member of the organisation.

It is worth noting that EU participation in international organisations constantly raises new challenges. One of these relates to the establishment of EU positions to be held within an international organisation or a body created by an international agreement.

[65] ECJ, Case C-45/07, *Commission v Greece* (IMO) [2009] ECR I-701, para 14.

[66] ibid, paras 16–20. Case 22/70 *Commission v Council* (AETR), [1971] ECR 263.

[67] ibid, paras 21–23.

[68] In *Commission v Sweden* (PFOS), the issue was similar to the one in the IMO case. A Member State brought its own proposal at the international level in a situation where a common position or a strategy of the Union was deemed to have been established, see ECJ, Case C-246/07 *Commission v Sweden* [2010] ECR I-3317, para 77.

[69] ECJ, *Opinion 2/91*, [1993] ECR I-1061, para 10; ECJ, *Opinion 1/03*, [2006] ECR I-1145, para 119. See also the subsequent case-law: Case C-459/03 *Commission v Ireland* [2006] ECR I-4635, para 174; Case C-246/07 *Commission v Sweden* (PFOS) [2010] ECR I-3317, para 69. In the doctrine, see M Fartunova-Michel and JF Delile (eds), *La coopération loyale dans le droit des relations extérieures de l'Union européenne, Collection Droit de l'Union européenne. Colloques* (Brussels, Bruylant, 2023); in a field of exclusive competence, see C Kaddous, 'L'impact du principe de coopération loyale sur la politique commerciale de l'Union', in that same book, 193–212.

B. Establishment of Positions to be Adopted on the EU's Behalf within an International Organisation

The establishment of EU positions was discussed many times in the case law of the Court in relation to the legality of the decision taken (eg in *Commission v Council*[70]) as well as to the conditions to be fulfilled by the EU under Article 218(9) TFEU to take such positions (*Germany v Council*[71] and more recently in the COTIF case[72]).

In *Commission v Council*, the legality of the Council decision establishing the position to be adopted on behalf of the European Community with regard to certain proposals submitted at a Conference of the parties to the CITES convention was challenged because the contested decision had been adopted without any mention of its legal basis. The failure to indicate any legal basis was not regarded as a purely formal defect and the decision was annulled.[73]

More interestingly, in the OIV case, Germany brought an action against the Council challenging the decision adopted pursuant to Article 218(9) TFEU establishing the position to be adopted on behalf of the EU with regard to specific resolutions to be voted in the framework of the International Organisation of Vine and Wine (OIV).[74] According to Germany, Article 218(9) TFEU was not the correct legal basis for the adoption of the contested decision, given that the provision only applies for the adoption of EU positions in bodies, set up by international agreements, of which the EU is a member. It contended, therefore, that the said provision could not be applied in relation to the representation of the Member States in bodies of international organisations in which only the Member States participate by virtue of separate international treaties.[75] In addition, the German government and the Member States which intervened in support of it claimed that Article 218(9) TFEU covers only 'acts having legal effects', which are meant

[70] ECJ, Case C-370/07, *Commission v Council* (CITES), [2009] ECR I-8917. CITES is the Convention on International Trade in Endangered Species of Wild Fauna and Flora.

[71] ECJ, Case C-399/12, *Germany v Council* (OIV), EU:C:2014:2258.

[72] ECJ, Case C-600/14, *Germany v Council* (COTIF), EU:C:2017:935.

[73] ECJ, Case C-370/07, *Commission v Council* (CITES) [2009] ECR I-8917, paras 61 and 62. However, the effects of the contested decision have been maintained on grounds of legal certainty, para 66.

[74] Council Document N° 11436 adopted on 18 June 2012 at the 2176 the Council meeting Agriculture and Fisheries, see Press Release 11179/12, p 16.

[75] Germany, supported by the Czech Republic, Luxembourg, Hungary, the Netherlands, Austria, the Slovak Republic and the United Kingdom, claimed that Article 218(9) TFEU was not applicable in the context of an international agreement which, like the OIV Agreement, had been concluded by the Member States and not by the European Union. ECJ, Case C-399/12, *Germany v Council* (OIV), EU:C:2014:258, para 29.

to be acts of international law being binding on the EU.[76] For Germany and its supporters, the OIV's recommendations did not fall within this category of acts referred to in Article 218(9).[77]

For its part, the Council, supported by the European Commission, contended first that Article 218(9) TFEU was applicable to the establishment of positions to be adopted on the EU's behalf in an organisation, such as the OIV, which was set up by an international agreement concluded by the Member States and which was called upon to adopt acts having legal effects, if the area in question fell within the competence of the EU.[78] According to the two institutions, Article 218(9) TFEU requires only that acts which the international body was called upon to adopt must have effects in the EU legal order; it is not necessary for those acts to produce effects in the international legal order.[79] Consequently, they maintained that the international recommendations relating to oenological practices and methods of analysis which were at stake, although non-binding, produced legal effects within the EU through the provisions of Union law which enforced them.[80]

This judgment is key as it deals with the challenges the EU and its Member States face in relation to participation in an international organisation. The Court first noted that Article 218(9) TFEU was making reference to a body set up by 'an agreement', but did not specify whether the EU had to be a party to that agreement. Similarly, the reference in that provision to the positions to be adopted 'on the Union's behalf' did not mean that the EU had to have been a party to the agreement which set up the international body in question. Consequently, the Court held that nothing in the wording of the Treaty prevented the EU from adopting a decision establishing a position to be adopted on its behalf in a body set up by an international agreement to which it was not a party.[81]

In that judgment, the Court stressed that the case concerned matters relating to the common agricultural policy and, more specifically, the common organisation of wine markets, an area which was regulated for the most part by the

[76] ECJ, Case C-399/12, *Germany v Council* (OIV), EU:C:2014:2258, paras 35 and 36.

[77] Article 218(9) TFEU reads as follows: 'The Council, on a proposal from the Commission or the High Representative of the Union for Foreign Affairs and Security Policy, shall adopt a decision suspending application of an agreement and establishing the positions to be adopted on the Union's behalf in a body set up by an agreement, when that body is called upon to adopt acts having legal effects, with the exception of acts supplementing or amending the institutional framework of the agreement'.

[78] ECJ, Case C-399/12, *Germany v Council* (OIV), EU:C:2014:2258, para 38.

[79] ECJ, Case C-399/12, *Germany v Council* (OIV), EU:C:2014:2258, para 44.

[80] ECJ, Case C-399/12, *Germany v Council* (OIV), EU:C:2014:2258, paras 45 and 46.

[81] ECJ, Case C-399/12, *Germany v Council* (OIV), EU:C:2014:2258, paras 49 and 50.

EU legislature in the exercise of its competence under Article 43 TFEU. This means that where an area of law falls within an EU competence, such as the one in question in the case, the fact that the EU does not take part in the international agreement in question does not prevent it from exercising that competence by establishing, through its institutions, a position to be adopted on its behalf in the body set up by that agreement, in particular through the Member States which are party to that agreement acting jointly in its interest.[82] Consequently, the fact that the EU was not a party to the OIV did not prevent the Court from applying Article 218(9) TFEU.

As to the other main argument brought by Germany, the Court checked whether the recommendations to be adopted by the OIV constituted 'acts having legal effects' for the purposes of Article 218(9). It appeared from the proceedings that those recommendations are taken into consideration for the purposes of drawing up rules of EU law. It followed that the recommendations were capable of decisively influencing the content of the legislation adopted by the EU legislature in the area of the common organisation of wine markets.[83] On this basis, the recommendations, in particular by reason of their incorporation into EU law by virtue of specific provisions of secondary legislation, had been regarded as having legal effects in that area for the purposes of Article 218(9) TFEU and the EU, while not a party to the OIV Agreement, was entitled to establish a position to be adopted on its behalf with regard to those recommendations, in view of their direct impact on the EU's *acquis* in that area.[84]

It follows from this OIV judgment that Article 218(9) TFEU applies for the establishment of positions to be adopted by the EU in an international organisation whether or not the EU as such participates in the said organisation. The possibility of an 'action' by the EU in an international organisation is therefore not prevented by the fact that it is not itself member of the organisation. Furthermore, the fact that only some of the Member States are members of the international organisation has no impact on their obligation to respect, present and defend the common position adopted by the EU and act jointly in the interest of the latter. The determining factor is the existence of an EU competence in the area concerned.

It can be recalled that in CFSP matters, Article 34 TEU provides expressly that in international organisations where not all the Member States participate,

[82] ECJ, Case C-399/12, *Germany v Council* (OIV), EU:C:2014:2258, paras 51 and 52. See also C-45/07 *Commission v Greece*, [2009] ECR I-701, paras 30 and 31; *Opinion 2/91*, [1993] ECR I-1061, para 5.

[83] ECJ, Case C-399/12, *Germany v Council* (OIV), EU:C:2014:2258, para 63.

[84] ECJ, Case C-399/12, *Germany v Council* (OIV), EU:C:2014:2258, para 64.

those which do take part must uphold the EU's positions. Furthermore, the Member States which are also members of the UN Security Council will defend the positions and the interests of the EU. Therefore, the judgment in the *Germany v Council* case actually presented no real surprise on the question of the consequences for the Member States which are parties to an international organisation. Only the question of the application of Article 218(9) TFEU had a specific legal interest. In the absence of a general provision governing all issues raised in connection with the participation of the EU in international organisations, the Court rightly gave an extensive interpretation of the Treaty provision in order to cover the situations where the EU is a member of the international organisation and those where it is not but has competence in the field of activity of the said organisation.

In the more recent COTIF case – which is known for the clarification brought by the Court of Justice on the possibility for the EU to exercise a shared competence by an EU-only agreement – Germany brought an action for the annulment of a Council decision adopted on the basis of Article 218(9) TFEU. The decision at stake defined the position the EU would hold at a Committee established by the Convention concerning International Carriage by Rail. Germany in that case mainly argued that the EU did not have the competence to adopt such a position under Article 218(9) TFEU as the EU can only act externally in the field of transport if it has previously acted internally. The Court dismissed this action. It stressed that the COTIF case differed from the one on the OIV as the EU is a member of COTIF along with all its Member States, with the exception of Malta and Cyprus. It also considered that the wording of Article 218(9) does not limit the action of the EU to situations where it has previously adopted internal rules in accordance with the ordinary legislative procedure.[85] In doing so, the Court admitted that Article 218(9) can also be applied to establish positions of the EU in areas where the EU has not previously acted internally.

The above examined cases clarified the meaning and scope of Article 218(9) TFEU. These clarifications increased the legal certainty in the field of the participation of the EU and its Member States in international organisations. This is welcomed in the interest of the EU and its Member States, but also in the interest of the other members of the international organisations that welcome more clarity on how the EU legal order functions.

[85] ECJ, Case C-600/14, *Germany v Council* (COTIF), EU:C:2017:935, para 71.

IV. Conclusion

The EU's engagement in multilateral fora is a multifaceted endeavour, entailing both internal challenges with its Member States and external dynamics with the other members of the international organisations. Guided by principles and rules enshrined in its Treaties, the EU aims to foster good governance in this realm

The evolution of the EU's external action, catalysed by the Lisbon Treaty, has led to a clearer international recognition of the EU's role. This transformation, which unified the European Community and the EU into one single entity, expanded the EU's activity on the global stage. By delineating the roles of various European actors, such as the President of the European Council, the President of the Commission, and the High Representative, the EU has bolstered its representation in international organisations.

As a global actor, the EU seeks to wield influence within international organisations either independently or jointly with its Member States. This necessitates cohesive action, as the EU's impact is maximised when it acts in the most 'united manner'. The principle of sincere cooperation, laid down in Article 4(3) TEU, underscores the importance of unity in the EU's engagement with international organisations, particularly in cases of 'mixed membership'.

Good governance in the EU's participation in international organisations hinges on coordination and sincere collaboration between EU institutions and Member States. Upholding the principles and rules governing this engagement is paramount, as they provide the foundation for legal certainty, both internally and externally, enabling the EU to effectively navigate the international arena.

2

The European Union and the Reform of the World Trade Organization

JOSEPHINE NORRIS AND FLAVIA MARISI*

I. Introduction

The World Trade Organization (WTO), which establishes the regulations for the multilateral trading system, currently consists of 164 States Parties,[1] and nearly 98 per cent of international trade takes place among these Members.[2]

Since the formation of the WTO's predecessor, the General Agreement on Tariffs and Trade (GATT), which was signed by 23 countries in 1947,[3] global trade has grown 300 times larger. In 2021, it accounted for approximately 56.5 per cent of the world's Gross Domestic Product (GDP),[4] contributing to job creation, economic expansion, innovation, and investment worldwide. Furthermore, this has facilitated consumers' access to a diverse range of products and services, while also promoting sustainable development globally by lifting hundreds of millions of people out of poverty.[5]

* The views expressed by the authors are personal and do not necessarily reflect an official position of the European Union, the European Commission or its Legal Service.

[1] World Trade Organization, 'Members and Observers', https://www.wto.org/english/thewto_e/whatis_e/tif_e/org6_e.htm.

[2] World Trade Organization, 'The WTO', https://www.wto.org/english/thewto_e/thewto_e.htm#:~:text=Membership,-Members%20and%20observers&text=The%20WTO%20has%20over%20160,per%20cent%20of%20world%20trade.

[3] Press Brief, 'Fiftieth Anniversary of the Multilateral Trading System', https://www.wto.org/english/thewto_e/minist_e/min96_e/chrono.htm.

[4] Macrotrends, 'World Trade to GDP Ratio 1970–2023', https://www.macrotrends.net/countries/WLD/world/trade-gdp-ratio#:~:text=Trade%20is%20the%20sum%20of,a%204.36%25%20increase%20from%202020.

[5] MGE Schaus, 'Reviving the WTO and Rules-Based Trading. The EU's role' (2022) 1 *CEPS Policy Insights* 1–2.

The system's stability plays a significant role in achieving these outcomes. The WTO implements the most-favoured-nation principle (MFN), which minimises discrimination against goods and services from various trading partners.[6] Furthermore, the binding of tariffs has reduced the likelihood of countries raising tariffs in response to economic shocks,[7] and the dispute settlement system is designed to ensure compliance with regulations and prevent the escalation of trade frictions into trade conflicts.

The WTO was established to fulfil three core functions that mutually support each other. Firstly, at the General Council level, the 'negotiating function' serves as a platform for trade liberalisation negotiations and the establishment of new rules. Secondly, the Trade Policy Review Body (TPRB) oversees and administers multilateral trade regulations and exercises a 'monitoring function'. Lastly, the Dispute Settlement Body (DSB) resolves trade disputes.[8]

Although the inherent nature of global economic governance would suggest that the WTO should be a significant actor, the WTO is widely perceived to be in 'crisis' and to lack relevance in the prevailing geopolitical context. Unfortunately, this ongoing crisis impacts all three functions of the WTO.

The WTO's process of creating new trade rules for twenty-first-century patterns of globalisation is burdensome and largely ineffective.[9] Additionally, the monitoring of trade policies lacks effectiveness.[10] The Dispute Settlement Method (DSM), which is considered its most valuable asset, faces unprecedented challenges due to the absence of the Appellate Body since December 2019. Negotiations have proven unsuccessful in updating the rules, resulting in the dispute settlement system reverting to a state reminiscent of the GATT era, where panel reports could be blocked. Furthermore, trade wars have resurfaced. Unsuitable rules and

[6] Reforming the WTO: Towards a Sustainable and Effective Multilateral Trading System, Annex to the Communication from the Commission to the European Parliament, the Council, the European Economic and Social Committee and the Committee of the Regions Trade Policy Review – An Open, Sustainable and Assertive Trade Policy, COM(2021) 66 final, 18.2.2021.

[7] A Jakubik and R Piermartini, 'How WTO commitments tame uncertainty!', *WTO Staff Working Papers* ERSD-2019-06 (World Trade Organization (WTO), 2019).

[8] M Schneider-Petsinger, *Reforming the World Trade Organization: Prospects for transatlantic cooperation and the global trade system*, Research Paper (London, Chatham House, 2020).

[9] ibid; B Hoekman, 'Urgent and Important: Improving WTO Performance by Revisiting Work Practices' (2019) 53(3) *Journal of World Trade* 373.

[10] Reforming the WTO: Towards a Sustainable and Effective Multilateral Trading System, Annex to the Communication from the Commission to the European Parliament, the Council, the European Economic and Social Committee and the Committee of the Regions 'Trade Policy Review – An Open, Sustainable and Assertive Trade Policy', COM(2021) 66 final, 18.2.2021.

prolonged dispute resolution lead countries to resort to unfair practices and may compel them to respond one-sidedly to safeguard their interests.[11]

Many WTO members, including the European Union, firmly believe that the WTO and global trade governance require significant reform.[12] The WTO itself acknowledges this to be the case. Yet, there is no universally agreed list of items on the WTO 'reform agenda'. The numerous disagreements relate to the specifics of the reform process, including how and what to reform, where to initiate the changes, and what should be prioritised. Indeed, individual members define the reform priorities very differently.[13]

Initially, the proposals for WTO reform primarily originated from developed countries, while developing countries were less actively involved in the reform process. The crisis relating to the Appellate Body in 2019 catalysed appetite for reform across a broad spectrum of the WTO's membership, and there now appears to be an emerging consensus that any reform process will have to be wide and deep. Among the various proposals, the EU proposal stands out as particularly comprehensive.[14] The WTO describes the issue of reform as 'broad' and presents the process as revolving around four areas of 'general concern': negotiating and concluding agreements; strengthening the work of the WTO bodies and committees; the adequacy of existing special and differential treatment provisions; and dispute settlement.[15]

In short, there are multiple areas within the WTO that require reform, and new rules are needed to establish stable, predictable, and fair global trade regulations that encompass the modern economy.[16] Nor is a progressive or piecemeal approach an option any longer. It has recently been argued that given the interconnected nature of the challenges that the WTO currently faces, efforts to revitalise multilateral trade cooperation would prove insufficient unless at least

[11] CR Willems, *Revitalizing the World Trade Organization* (Atlantic Council Geoeconomic Center October 2020): https://www.atlanticcouncil.org/in-depth-research-reports/report/revitalizing-the-wto/.

[12] J Wouters and V Hegde, 'Reform of global trade governance: the role of the European Union' (2022) 44(5) *Journal of European Integration* 715–30.

[13] As of 2022, the WTO had received over 30 submissions addressing the question of reform.

[14] S Jelisavac Trošić, 'What is the Role of the European Union in Reshaping the Future of the World Trade Organization?' in K Zakić and B Demirtaş (eds), *Europe in changes: The old continent at a new crossroads* (Institute of International Politics and Economics, Belgrade Faculty of Security Studies at the University of Belgrade, 2021).

[15] WTO 12th Ministerial Conference, MC12 Briefing Note: WTO Reform: https://www.wto.org/english/thewto_e/minist_e/mc12_e/briefing_notes_e/bfwtoreform_e.htm.

[16] J Caporal, W Reinsch, M Waddoups and C Tassin de Montaigu, *The WTO at a Crossroad* (Center for Strategic & International Studies, September 2019): https://www.csis.org/analysis/wto-crossroad.

the WTO's negotiating function and dispute settlement mechanism are addressed in parallel.[17]

The EU, as a significant global trading bloc, has a clear strategic interest in international trade and adherence to the rules that apply to the international trading system. It seeks to play a leading role in shaping the discussions around the future of the WTO. This chapter first briefly examines the main functions of the WTO and the reasons why there is a widespread belief that all three functions need to be modernised and optimised. It then considers the role and influence of the EU as an actor in that process.

II. The WTO Reform Agenda

A. The Negotiating Function

Whilst the negotiating function of the WTO is often identified as a core pillar of its activity, it is an aspect of the WTO's mandate which has, to date, yielded limited output. In the 28 years since the establishment of the WTO, only two new agreements have been successfully concluded: the Trade Facilitation Agreement[18] and the WTO Agreement on Fisheries Subsidies.[19] Only the first of these has entered into force. Other negotiations did not fare as well. The negotiations for the plurilateral Trade in Services Agreement (TiSA), initiated in March 2013, failed in November 2016. Similarly, negotiations for the plurilateral Environmental Goods Agreement (EGA), launched in 2014, also failed in 2016. In contrast, the range of substantive issues in respect of which members are calling either for new rules or for a review of the existing WTO regulatory framework has increased exponentially in recent years. This growing backlog of substantive issues awaiting a plurilateral solution reinforces the perception that the WTO simply cannot deliver on its negotiating function without revitalisation and reform.

The different reasons for the accumulation of this 'backlog' frame the discussions on what this reform should entail.

[17] B Hoekman and PC Mavroidis, 'WTO Reform: Back to the Past to Build for the Future' (2021) 12(53) *Global Policy* 5–12.

[18] WTO, Protocol Amending the Marrakesh Agreement Establishing the World Trade Organization Decision of 27 November 2014, WT/L/940, 28 November 2014.

[19] WTO, Agreement on Fisheries Subsidies, Ministerial Decision of 17 June 2022, WT/MIN(22)/33 WT/L/1144, 22 June 2022.

First, there is the question of the speed with which the WTO is able to adapt. The scale and the scope of (potential) reform are, to a degree, dictated by the nature of the underlying drivers of change. Since 1995, the geopolitical context has shifted considerably. Emerging technologies together with new global priorities, such as climate change mitigation and fears over security of supply, have prompted a dramatic alteration in trade practices among the membership. Some events, such as the Covid 19 pandemic, were unprecedented and unforeseeable. Others, such as the development of global value chains, have emerged more gradually but have increased vulnerabilities to trade shocks. The trading practices deployed by members to respond to these new global realities have not been reflected in modifications to the rules. In other words, the WTO's negotiating function has been outpaced.[20]

To truly reform the WTO, it is therefore crucial to modernising its trade rules to reflect these shifts in global economic power and technological advancements.[21] Specifically, new rules should be established to govern digital trade, investment and services. All three areas of negotiation are vital for adapting international trade rules to the digital transformation of the economy, facilitating investment as a key driver of development, and recognising the growing significance of digital services.[22] Changes in trade patterns, such as global value chains, foreign direct investments, services and e-commerce, as well as aligning trade with sustainability objectives, – particularly environmental sustainability – must also be addressed.

Second, there is an issue of obsolescence. Some aspects of international trade already subject to the disciplines of the WTO have simply been overtaken by global economic developments. Market access commitments have not been updated since the conclusion of the Uruguay Round in 1995, whereas the global economy has evolved considerably in the intervening period. The widening 'gap' between economic realities in 1995 and those which exist now is providing a strong impetus for negotiations to 'level the playing-field'. Hence, the existing rulebook needs to be re-examined where it has become outdated.

[20] In a Concept Paper on WTO Reform, the EU summarised the situation as follow: 'In essence, since 1995 the world has changed; the WTO has not.' See European Commission, 'WTO modernisation. Introduction to future EU proposals' (18 September 2018), available on the website of the Directorate General for Trade: The EU and the WTO (europa.eu).

[21] Schneider-Petsinger (n 8 above).

[22] Reforming The WTO: Towards a Sustainable and Effective Multilateral Trading System, Annex to the Communication from the Commission to the European Parliament, the Council, the European Economic and Social Committee and the Committee of the Regions Trade Policy Review – An Open, Sustainable and Assertive Trade Policy, COM(2021) 66 final, 18.2.2021.

Whether due to an inability to adapt sufficiently fast or to a lack of flexibility to adjust existing rules, in many cases the need for WTO reform can be linked to an identifiable global change or to an alteration in trading practices associated with such a change.

One example is the impact of technological progress. At present, existing WTO rules do not adequately address the implications of new technologies. The organisation lacks rules governing internet-based trade, e-commerce, cybersecurity, and data residency.[23] The need for a fundamental review of the rules on digital trade and services is, therefore, directly linked to the use of emerging technologies and the digital transformation. This is undoubtedly a fast-paced regulatory environment which raises complex and highly technical issues. Even allowing for this, progress at the level of the WTO to react to these challenges is perceived to have been painfully and unacceptably slow.

Subsidies reform is an example of an item on the agenda which can be linked to a change in trade practices. According to studies, subsidies of one type or another constitute the great majority of trade interventions imposed since 2009.[24] Industrial subsidies, whether to support climate change mitigation measures or to counteract the effects of the Covid 19 pandemic, have proliferated even while tariffs have been reduced. But although subsidies are now a primary means through which local production is being supported, this is simply not fully captured by the existing rulebook. As a result, members are pushing for a revision of the Agreement on Subsidies and Countervailing Measures (SCM Agreement). The EU has argued, for instance, that the definition of 'prohibited subsidies' should be revised and expanded. Moreover, it has been argued that reforms should target trade-distorting practices linked to substantial state involvement in the economy.[25]

However, some items have been on the 'reform agenda' for such a long period that the rate of global developments is plainly insufficient to explain the failure of the WTO to deliver solutions. Arguably, it is these areas of prospective reform which provide the greatest insights into what elements of the negotiating function require modification, as opposed to more resources or more political commitment from the membership.

Agriculture is a case in point. It is a core interest for much of the WTO membership, yet members have been discussing agricultural trade reform since

[23] Willems (n 11 above).
[24] SJ Evenett and J Fritz, *Subsidies and Market Access: Towards an Inventory of Corporate Subsidies by China, the European Union and the United States* (London, CEPR Press, 2021).
[25] Schaus (n 5 above).

the Uruguay Round. Whilst those discussions have stagnated, the need to achieve progress is increasing as linkages with other policy areas are reinforced. For example, the impact of the climate change agenda on agriculture together with the emerging global food crisis are placing significant additional pressure on the system. Positions within the membership are polarised around issues such as 'special and differential treatment', market access commitments, and changes to the rules relating to agricultural subsidies.

The WTO's ability to keep pace with global change is clearly not the main issue hampering its negotiating function in this area. Rather the inability to bridge the divides and make progress is indicative of overarching structural and procedural factors.

It has been suggested that, on a fundamental level, within the WTO there is an absence of suitable structures for negotiations, commensurate with the complexities of the subject-matter to be negotiated.[26] The system for negotiation has been described by the EU as 'antiquated'.[27] Indeed, whilst the scope of trade issues covered by the WTO has been expanded – for instance to include intellectual property and government procurement – the underlying institutional framework has not evolved significantly since its inception.

The WTO primarily operates based on the 'single undertaking' principle, which means that nothing is agreed upon until everything is agreed upon. Moreover, decisions are made by consensus, making it challenging to reach agreement among all WTO members for a new multilateral initiative. In that sense, just as the broad membership of the WTO has been key to its success, it is an element which has impacted its ability to deliver on its negotiating mandate. However, it is also true that this approach, although rendering it more difficult to reach agreement, ensures that decisions are more likely to be acceptable to all members. In response to the difficulties in achieving consensus, one of the EU proposals for reform is to introduce a simplified process for amending existing agreements.

Equally, existing structures do not readily offer a platform to integrate horizontal issues, such as the reconciliation of trade liberalisation and the environment. Committees tend to negotiate in silos. In a context of increasing interlinkages and interdependencies between different items on the reform agenda, this makes solutions far more complex to achieve.

[26] See T Cottier, 'Preparing for Structural Reform in the WTO' (World Trade Institute, Berne, 26 September 2006), https://www.wto.org/english/forums_e/public_forum_e/structural_reform_of_the_wto_cottier.pdf.

[27] See EU Concept Paper on WTO Reform (n 20 above).

The failure of WTO negotiations to update international trade rules can be contrasted with the negotiations that have led to the conclusion of various Free Trade Agreements (FTAs). The list of comparative shortcomings is long. For instance, important areas such as intellectual property and services, which are governed by the high standards set in modern FTAs have not been matched with equivalent commitments in the WTO. Similarly, the WTO has yet to effectively tackle politically significant policy issues like labour and the environment, which are crucial for maintaining domestic support for the WTO as an institution.[28] Modern FTAs, including those negotiated by the EU, *do* address these issues. For example, in 2022 the EU announced that it has upgraded the trade and sustainable development chapters in its future FTAs.

Due to the difficulties of concluding comprehensive multilateral negotiations, countries have increasingly turned to bilateral or regional negotiations, involving subsets of WTO members and often focusing on specific sectors. These plurilateral negotiations aim to establish new agreements known as Joint Statement Initiatives (JSIs).[29] This approach has gained popularity among certain WTO members, including the EU, as it is based on alliances among like-minded countries, reducing the risk of individual countries attempting to advance specific agendas through 'hostage-taking'. Furthermore, plurilateral agreements, like FTAs, can facilitate the expansion of rules into new areas.[30]

The hope is that plurilateral negotiations can potentially yield tangible outcomes within reasonable time-frames and contribute to the development of stronger legal frameworks within the WTO.[31] It is worth noting that the WTO 'Marrakech Agreement' allows for the integration of plurilateral agreements into its legal structure, as outlined in Article X:9.[32] This provision enables the Ministerial Conference, through consensus, to include trade agreements concluded by a group of WTO members in the list of WTO plurilateral agreements found in Annex 4 to the Agreement.[33] However, it is important to acknowledge that Article X:9 has remained unused since the establishment of the WTO.

[28] Willems (n 11 above).
[29] WTO, 'Joint Statement Initiatives': https://www.wto.org/english/tratop_e/jsi_e/jsi_e.htm.
[30] Schneider-Petsinger (n 8 above).
[31] Schaus (n 5 above).
[32] WTO Agreement – Article X:9.
[33] WTO Agreement, Annex 4 Plurilateral Trade Agreements, https://www.wto.org/english/docs_e/legal_e/30-pluri.pdf; Reforming the WTO: Towards a Sustainable and Effective Multilateral Trading System, Annex to the Communication from the Commission to the European Parliament, the Council, the European Economic and Social Committee and the Committee of the Regions Trade Policy Review – An Open, Sustainable and Assertive Trade Policy, COM(2021) 66 final, 18.2.2021.

On the downside, expanding bilateral and regional Free Trade Agreements beyond the scope of WTO multilateral rules heightens the risk of regulatory inconsistencies.[34] The proliferation of such agreements has led to what is commonly referred to as the 'spaghetti bowl effect',[35] where multiple intersecting and potentially conflicting agreements hinder trade instead of facilitating and promoting it. Furthermore, bilateral or regional Free Trade Agreements can discourage participation in multilateral negotiations. As noted by India and South Africa, through JSIs, WTO Members may circumvent the fundamental principles and procedures of the WTO Agreement based on consensus.[36]

Consequently, the current situation raises concerns about the potential loss of legitimacy for the WTO, as, in the view of some researchers, influential States Parties disregard its rules and gravitate towards unilateralism and economic nationalism.[37]

Hence, structural changes to the WTO's negotiating function are essential both to allow negotiations on substantive issues to yield results within a reasonable time-frame (or, arguably, to facilitate the emergence of negotiated outcomes at all) and, critically, to preserve the relevance of the WTO in this pillar of activity.

B. Monitoring and Deliberative Functions

One of the functions of the WTO, as identified in Article III:1 of the Marrakesh Agreement, is to 'facilitate the implementation, administration and operation, and further the objectives' of the WTO Agreements. The second pillar of the WTO's core activities relates to this deliberative function – namely the space it offers through the committees and other fora for the membership to discuss issues and develop approaches to trade policy. Linked to this is the role and function of the WTO Secretariat in monitoring trade developments across the membership.

The monitoring of trade policies is one of the key functions of the WTO, carried out by the TPRB, a subsidiary body of the General Council, established through the Marrakesh Agreement. The TPRB is responsible for various functions, including monitoring, deliberation, committee activities, and promoting

[34] Schneider-Petsinger (n 8 above).

[35] J Bhagwati, 'US Trade Policy: The Infatuation with Free Trade Agreements', in J Bhagwati and A Krueger (eds), *The Dangerous Drift to Preferential Trade Agreements* (Washington DC, AEI Press, 1995).

[36] World Trade Organization, *The Legal Status of 'Joint Statement Initiatives' and their Negotiated Outcomes*, WT/GC/W/819 (19 February 2021).

[37] R Bowen and JL Broz, *Designing An International Economic Order: A Research Agenda* (Working Paper 27914, National Bureau of Economic Research, 2020).

transparency. Its main role is to administer the Trade Policy Review Mechanism (TPRM). The TPRM's purpose is to enhance States Parties' adherence to the rules, disciplines, and commitments established under the Multilateral Trade Agreements, as well as relevant Plurilateral Trade Agreements. By achieving greater transparency and understanding of the trade policies and practices of WTO members, the TPRM aims to contribute to the smoother functioning of the multilateral trading system.[38]

Under this function, all WTO Members may put questions to other WTO Members about the latter's policies and legislation. This helps the former to gather more information and have clarity on whether they intend to launch a formal dispute settlement procedure. However, it is evident that this function of the TPRB is currently underperforming and does not offer significant usefulness.

The existing WTO Agreements include transparency and notification requirements as essential components. However, the WTO system essentially relies on members to adhere to those transparency mechanisms and to inform the membership of any measures they have adopted. Although transparency and notification obligations are meant to provide factual information about each member's implementation of the relevant agreements,[39] in practice, many WTO members fail to adhere to them. Compliance with these requirements has been consistently low and delayed.[40]

This lack of adherence poses significant challenges, as compliance with these obligations is crucial to accurately understand the current legal framework, identify practices that might distort trade, and ensure members' adherence to their commitments.[41] The low rate of notifications, especially under certain agreements such as the Agreement on the Application of Sanitary and Phytosanitary Measures (SPS) and the Technical Barriers to Trade Agreement (TBT),[42] dents trust in the international trade system, and at the same time undermines predictability in

[38] World Trade Organization, 'The Trade Policy Review Mechanism (TPRM)', https://www.wto.org/english/tratop_e/tpr_e/tprm_e.htm.

[39] 'Procedures to Enhance Transparency and Strengthen Notification Requirements under WTO Agreements', Communication from the United States to the WTO Council for Trade in Goods, 30 October 2017, https://tinyurl.com/y3w6xgb4.

[40] See the WTO Secretariat's 'Annual Report on Notifications' provided to the Council for Trade in Goods. The most recent version is the following: World Trade Organization, 'Updating of the Listing of Notification Obligations and the Compliance therewith as Set out in Annex III of the Report of the Working Group on Notification Obligations and Procedures', Revision 30, 14 February 2023, https://docs.wto.org/dol2fe/Pages/SS/directdoc.aspx?filename=q:/G/L/223R30.pdf&Open=True.

[41] See 'Report of the Committee on Subsidies and Countervailing Measures', World Trade Organization, 23 October 2018, https://tinyurl.com/ y3oolz77.

[42] MB Karttunen, *Transparency in the WTO SPS and TBT Agreements: The Real Jewel in the Crown* (Cambridge, Cambridge University Press, 2020), 217–93.

international trade.[43] A particular systemic problem is the low rates of compliance with notification requirements related to subsidies, State-Owned Enterprises (SOEs), and safeguard measures.[44] This non-compliance has implications for future negotiations as well, as it creates ambiguity about the adherence to existing rules, making it difficult to establish new ones.[45]

As a result, a growing number of members consider that reliance on members for notification alone is insufficient. One potential solution is that the WTO Secretariat should be accorded a greater role in the monitoring process. The EU, for example, has specifically proposed increasing the incentives for compliance with notification requirements and imposing sanctions for repeated non-compliance. Equally, it has been suggested that the typology of measures that are required to be notified should be expanded, for instance to cover all aspects of trade and investment in services. Another 'gap' in the scope of notification requirements relates to the so-called 'general economic support' measures. The existing, limited methods available to the Secretariat to obtain information from members on this type of measure have been described as yielding 'dismal' results,[46] yet the overall importance of such measures in global trade dynamics continues to increase.

C. Special and Differential Treatment

Under the current rules, WTO members self-designate as 'developing countries'. This status is a precondition for eligibility for 'special and differential treatment', which grants them more favourable terms or additional time in which to meet their obligations. Indeed, the WTO's agreements contain over 150 provisions for developing countries and Least Developed Countries (LDCs). This includes access to technical assistance activities and longer transition periods to implement agreements and decisions.[47] As a result, it is unsurprising that approximately two-thirds of WTO members claim developing country status.[48]

[43] Willems (n 11).

[44] World Trade organization, 'Minutes of the Regular Meeting Held on 24 October 2017' (January 2018), https://docs.wto.org/dol2fe/Pages/FE_Search/FE_S_S009-DP.aspx?language=E&CatalogueIdList=241717,241617,238057,238041,233838,233839,230431,230450,226785,226642&CurrentCatalogueIdIndex=0&FullTextHash=&HasEnglishRecord=True&HasFrenchRecord=False&HasSpanishRecord=False.

[45] Schneider-Petsinger (n 8 above).

[46] B Hoekman, X Tu and R Wolfe, *China and WTO reform* (EUI RSC Working Paper 2022/59).

[47] For an analysis by the WTO Secretariat, see 'Special and Differential Treatment Provisions in WTO Agreements and Decisions' (October 2018), WT/COMTD/W/239.

[48] World Trade Organization (undated), 'Understanding the WTO: Developing Countries', https://www.wto.org/english/thewto_e/whatis_e/tif_e/dev1_e.htm.

However, there is no agreed definition of a developing country within the WTO, nor are there objective criteria in the WTO system to determine when a member is entitled to be recognised as such.[49] Self-declaration of developing country status is not governed by any specific guidelines such as the country's share of global trade or sectoral competitiveness.[50]

This has resulted in a situation where some of the wealthiest economies, such as Brunei, Hong Kong, Kuwait, Macao, Qatar, and the United Arab Emirates, are classified as developing countries within the WTO. Additionally, eight G20 countries, namely Argentina, China, India, Indonesia, Mexico, Saudi Arabia, South Africa, and Turkey, are considered developing countries despite their significant economic size. Two of them, China and India, are among the four largest economies globally, whereas Mexico and Turkey are members of the Organisation for Economic Co-operation and Development (OECD).

The capacity for prominent emerging economies to categorise themselves as developing countries and consequently benefit from certain exemptions is economically perplexing and places the least developed countries (LDCs) at a disadvantage, as they are frequently grouped together with the large emerging economies despite their genuine need for special considerations. Additionally, some nations assert that trade liberalisation and the regulations promoting it, which are central to the mission of the WTO, impede development instead of fostering it.[51]

Resolving this issue is seen as essential in order to make progress on other aspects of reform including many of the negotiations on substantive trade policy. For example, it was the inability of the membership to agree on exemptions for developing countries that proved problematic in the context of the negotiations of the Agreement on Fisheries Subsidies and which ultimately resulted in the conclusion of an agreement with a significantly reduced substantive reach compared to that initially contemplated.

The US proposed an end to the system of self-designation of 'developing country status' in 2019. The EU is also among those WTO members who are advocating for a change to the current system, specifically to modify clauses providing for open-ended block exemptions toward a needs-driven and evidence-based approach. The EU has also argued in favour of 'graduation'. The question of how to

[49] Willems (n 11).
[50] World Trade Organization (undated), 'Who are the developing countries in the WTO?', https://www.wto. org/english/tratop_e/devel_e/d1who_e.htm.
[51] Willems (n 11 above).

address 'special and differential treatment' remains particularly divisive amongst the membership. For instance, in 2019, China, India and nine other members circulated a paper emphasising the continued existence of the development divide and insisting on the role of self-designation as a 'developing country'.[52] A common position remains elusive.

D. Dispute Settlement and the Paralysis of the Appellate Body

Resolving trade disputes is the third core pillar of the WTO's activities. It complements and is arguably essential to ensure the overall functioning of the covered agreements. Indeed, as has been cogently argued, the value of negotiated outcomes depends on the ability of signatories to enforce them.[53]

The Dispute Settlement Body (DSB) has successfully resolved over 600 cases to date. It is structured around a two-tier system, with disputes initially heard by a Panel. The highest instance forum in international trade dispute settlement is the Appellate Body, which consists of seven adjudicators responsible for hearing appeals on panel reports issued in disputes between WTO members. Appeals can be brought forward by countries that disagree with the findings of the panel.

As has been highlighted by the EU, the Appellate Body has significantly contributed to the legitimacy and predictability of the WTO dispute settlement system. It has thoroughly considered issues such as the protection of WTO members' rights to regulate for health, environment, and other legitimate policy objectives. Furthermore, it safeguards both large and small WTO members against unjustified trade-restrictive measures and avoids any potential intensification of trade disputes into political hostilities.[54]

In 2016, the United States, which had been voicing criticisms in relation to WTO dispute settlement for some time, decided to disengage and refused to agree to the appointment of new members to the Appellate Body. The final collapse of the two-tier dispute settlement system occurred in 2019 when the terms of existing

[52] See WT/GC/W/765/Rev.2. 4 March 2019.

[53] B Hoekman and PC Mavroidis, 'WTO Reform: Back to the Past to Build for the Future' (2021) 12 *Global Policy* 5–12.

[54] Reforming The WTO: Towards a Sustainable and Effective Multilateral Trading System, Annex to the Communication from the Commission to the European Parliament, the Council, the European Economic and Social Committee and the Committee of the Regions Trade Policy Review – An Open, Sustainable and Assertive Trade Policy, COM(2021) 66 final, 18.2.2021.

Appellate Body members expired, resulting in a lack of quorum for that body to hear new disputes.

As a result, when parties file appeals against panel decisions, they now face a 'void'. Consequently, panel reports under appeal cannot be adopted by the DSB, leaving these disputes in limbo. This situation frustrates the very purpose of the Dispute Settlement System (DSS) as any domestic measure challenged as inconsistent with WTO rules remains in place,[55] even where there has been a favourable panel report and recommendations have been made. It has been suggested that the problem with the current single-tier DSS surviving without an Appellate Body is that it creates uncertainty regarding the outcomes of trade disputes.[56] Until the Appellate Body becomes operational again, the disputing parties must either wait, or find an agreed solution themselves.[57]

A further possible outcome is that, instead of waiting indefinitely, parties who succeed at the Panel stage are prone to take the initiative and adopt retaliatory measures. This could result in increased unilateralism, protectionism, and a shift towards power dynamics rather than rule-based trade relations.[58] In essence, this could bring an end to the WTO's system of dispute resolution.[59] This move by the US has, therefore, arguably undermined the relevance of the DSB itself.

Whilst the need for reform of the dispute settlement structures has become particularly pressing since the cessation of the functioning of the Appellate Body in 2019, issues relating to the general functioning of the WTO dispute settlement mechanism are more long-standing.[60] Presented by the US as 'systemic concerns', core criticisms relate to non-adherence to time-frames,[61] the scope of

[55] G Sacerdoti, *The WTO Dispute Settlement System in 2020: Facing the Appellate Body Paralysis* (Bocconi Legal Studies Research Paper Series, research paper no 3794327, February 2021).

[56] A Raina, 'Meditations in an Emergency: The Appellate Body Deadlock – What It Is, Why It Is a Problem, and What to Do About It' (2018) 13(9) *Global Trade and Customs Journal* 376–86; J Galbraith, 'United States Continues to Block New Appellate Body Members for the World Trade Organization, Risking the Collapse of the Appellate Process' (2019) 113(4) *American Journal of International Law* 822–31; J Hillman, 'Three Approaches to Fixing the World Trade Organization's Appellate Body: The Good, the Bad and the Ugly?', Institute for International Economic Law, Georgetown University Law Center, 2018, https://www.law.georgetown.edu/wp-content/uploads/ 2018/12/Hillman-Good-Bad-Ugly-Fix-to-WTO-Appellate Body.pdf.

[57] O Starshinova, 'Is the MPIA a Solution to the WTO Appellate Body Crisis?' (2021) 55(5) *Journal of World Trade* 787–803, 800.

[58] Schneider-Petsinger (n 8).

[59] CP Bown, 'The 2018 Trade War and the End of Dispute Settlement as we knew it' in MA Crowley (ed), *Trade War: The Clash of Economic Systems Endangering Global Prosperity* (CEPR Press, 2019) 21–32.

[60] M Fiorini, B Hoekman, PC Mavroidis, M Saluste and R Wolfe, 'WTO Dispute Settlement and the Appellate Body: Insider Perceptions and Members' Revealed Preferences' (2020) 54(5) *Journal of World Trade* 667–98.

[61] For example, the US has criticised the Appellate Body on the grounds that it has disregarded multiple times the rule under Article 17.5 of the Understanding on Rules and Procedures Governing

the Appellate Body's mandate, a perceived tendency on the part of the Appellate Body to make findings beyond the scope of the dispute,[62] and the extent to which Appellate Body reports may be considered to establish precedent over subsequent Panel findings.[63] Moreover, some members, most notably the US, consider that certain issues, such as essential security concerns, should fall entirely outside the scope of legal review.[64] That position is not shared by the EU.

The EU has consistently highlighted dispute settlement in general and a return to a functioning Appellate Body as a priority area of reform.[65] As preserving a second level of legal review can enhance the credibility of reports and prevent significant legal errors by Panels,[66] a growing percentage of the membership, as well as many external stakeholders, share this position. However, although one of the outcomes of the 12th Ministerial Conference in 2022 was a commitment by the members to 'conduct discussions with the view to having a fully and well-functioning dispute settlement system accessible to all Members by 2024',[67] progress in reaching a substantive agreement has been less rapid than hoped for.

E. The Issue of Market Economy Status

At its inception in 1947, the GATT, which later evolved into the WTO, did not incorporate explicit guidelines for determining a country's market economy status. The original members of GATT operated under the assumption that all participants would uphold the principles of a liberal economic system. However, this assumption remained implicit and was not formally articulated within the GATT/WTO Agreements.[68]

the Settlement of Disputes (DSU), which requires it to issue reports within 90 days of any appeal, irrespective of whether the disputing members have agreed to an extension.

[62] See Office of the United States Trade Representative, *Report on the Appellate Body of the World Trade Organization*, February 2020, https://ustr.gov/sites/default/files/Report_on_the_Appellate_Body_of_the_World_Trade_Organization.pdf, 26–32.

[63] See MC de Andrade, 'Precedent in the WTO: Retrospective Reflections for a Prospective Dispute Settlement Mechanism' (2020) 11(2) *Journal of International Dispute Settlement* 262.

[64] See US Statement following the Panel Reports in DS544 of 27 January 2023, Statements by the United States at the Meeting of the WTO Dispute Settlement Body | United States Trade Representative (ustr.gov).

[65] See for instance, Council conclusions at the start of the 12th World Trade Organization Ministerial Conference, 12 June 2022.

[66] Willems (n 11 above).

[67] MC12 Outcome Document, 17 June 2022, WT/MIN(22)/24 WT/L/1135.

[68] PC Mavroidis and A Sapir, *China and the World Trade Organisation: Towards a better fit*, Working paper, issue 06/2019 (Bruegel, June 2019).

Since its establishment, the multilateral trade system has welcomed countries with economic systems that differ from liberalism. The WTO acknowledges the members' right to determine the characteristics of a market economy on their own. This was exemplified by the inclusion of command economies like Yugoslavia, Poland, Romania, and Hungary, which joined the WTO in 1966, 1967, 1971, and 1973, respectively.[69] These centrally planned economies were traditionally classified as non-market economies (NMEs). Their incompatibility with market economy principles was addressed through accession protocols, in which they committed to respect certain rules and principles.

Similarly, China also became a member of the WTO through an accession protocol.[70] Currently, China argues that the language used in its WTO accession protocol obliges other members to cease treating China as an NME when calculating margins in 'anti-dumping' proceedings after December 2016.[71] In fact, more than 80 countries, including Australia, Chile, New Zealand, Peru, and South Africa, recognise China as a market economy. However, when assessing anti-dumping duties, the US and the EU continue to classify China as an NME.[72]

This discrepancy arises from Article 15(d) of China's Accession Protocol, which stipulates that in order to be considered a market economy in anti-dumping proceedings, China must establish that it is a market economy under the importing WTO member's national law, provided that the latter includes market economy criteria as of the date of accession. The EU uses its own criteria, such as the liberalisation of prices and the existence of an effective business framework, to determine China's market economy status. Instead, the US criteria include wage liberalisation and market access for foreign direct investment.[73]

[69] WTO, 'The 128 countries that had signed GATT by 1994', https://www.wto.org/english/thewto_e/gattmem_e.htm.

[70] WTO, Accession of The People's Republic of China, Decision of 10 November 2001, WT/L/432 23 November 2001.

[71] If an exporter sets the price of an exported product at a price that is lower than the price for the same goods under normal conditions of trade when sold domestically in the exporting country, it is considered to be 'dumping' that product. In anti-dumping investigations in the European Union, the method for calculating dumping margins varies, based on whether the exporting country is classified as a market economy or a non-market economy (NME). Typically, NME methodologies result in higher anti-dumping duties.

[72] Schneider-Petsinger (n 8); European Parliamentary Research Service, 'Calculation of dumping margins – EU and US rules and practices in light of the debate on China's Market Economy Status', March 2016, https://www.europarl.europa.eu/RegData/etudes/IDAN/2016/583794/EPRS_IDA(2016)583794_EN.pdf.

[73] B Stefanova and P Zhelev, 'Revisiting China's market economy status: state capitalism within the WTO liberal trading system' (2022) 114(2) *Australian and New Zealand Journal of European Studies* 94–111.

The divergence in criteria for defining a market economy also contributes to the differing views between the EU, the US, and China regarding China's market economy/NME status. China has taken measures to shift away from centralised planning and has actively engaged in the promotion of trade liberalisation on the global stage. This demonstrates a convergence of its economic openness with that of well-established market economies. However, China also adheres to a model of restricted reciprocity concerning market entry, investment, and ownership. This approach may endure due to the varying frameworks of economic governance, which result in distinctions between state-owned and privately-owned economic entities.[74]

F. State Involvement in a Country's Economy

The involvement of the state in the economies of certain WTO members presents a significant challenge to the organisation. Those economic systems, characterised by heavy state intervention, restrict market access and have negative effects on global markets. Unfair trade and investment practices may include heavy subsidisation for industrial policy objectives, leading to excess capacities and negative spill-overs across borders. Coercive practices like forced technology transfers and the support of SOEs that prioritise government objectives over market corrections also contribute to these challenges.[75]

China, in particular, has faced criticism from the US and other WTO members due to its widespread use of subsidies to and through SOEs. Other members complain that these practices create an uneven playing-field among WTO members and distort international competition. The existing WTO rules have not fully and effectively addressed these trade-distortive practices, including the provisions outlined in China's Accession Protocol to the WTO.[76]

In spite of initiating early measures to transition towards a market-based economy, China's level of trade and investment openness continues to be relatively limited considering its substantial global economic impact.[77] Furthermore,

[74] ibid.

[75] J Pelkmans and J François (coord), *Tomorrow's Silk Road: Assessing an EU-China Free Trade Agreement* (CEPS, Brussels and Rowman & Littlefield International, London, 2018).

[76] G Sacerdoti, *The WTO Dispute Settlement System in 2020: Facing the Appellate Body Paralysis*, Bocconi Legal Studies Research Paper Series, research paper no 3794327 (2021).

[77] European Commission, *Reforming the WTO: Towards a Sustainable and Effective Multilateral Trading System*, Annex to the Communication, COM(2021) 66, 18 February 2021, at 1–2.

China has not only rolled back certain reforms but has also encountered difficulties in successfully implementing others.[78] The presence of SOEs in China presents a significant obstacle to the global trading system. While their actions may not exhibit discriminatory behaviour, they often prioritise non-commercial considerations, resulting in significant distortions within the market.[79]

Certain analysts contend that China's economic model, which is characterised by significant state intervention and control, poses a formidable obstacle to the liberal international order that is built upon the principles of the WTO.[80]

III. The EU as an Actor in the WTO Reform Process

The EU, a full member of the WTO since its inception in 1995, has taken an active role within the organisation from the outset. This is reflected in the EU's participation in the WTO's policy-making and negotiation functions; for instance the EU was a driving force behind the discussions leading to the Doha Round (2001–08). It is also illustrated by the EU's use of the WTO dispute settlement mechanism; according to statistics compiled by the WTO, as of May 2023, the EU has participated as a complainant in 110 disputes, as a defendant in 92 disputes and as a third party in 216 disputes. Equally, the EU is the largest contributor to the WTO budget, accounting for more than 30 per cent of contributions.[81]

Given this prominence, it is unsurprising that in the context of the discussions relating to the reform process, the EU has also sought to ascribe to itself a 'leading role'. Indeed, the EU has identified this leadership function as being essential from a trade-policy perspective.[82]

There are several factors which explain this positioning by the EU.

[78] Schaus (n 5).

[79] Schaus (n 5).

[80] S Ezell, 'False promises II: The continuing gap between China's WTO commitments and its practice'. Information Technology & Innovation Foundation (26 July 2021), https://www2.itif.org/2021-false-promises.pdf; MT Hošman, 'China's NME status at the WTO: Analysis of the debate' (2021) 20(1) *Journal of International Trade Law and Policy* 1–20; J Pelkmans, 'China's "Socialist Market Economy": A Systemic Trade Issue' (2018) 53 *Intereconomics* 268–73.

[81] See WTO 2021: Annual Report 2021 (wto.org).

[82] See Annex to the Communication from the Commission to the European Parliament, the Council, the European Economic and Social Committee and the Committee of the Regions – Trade Policy Review – An Open, Sustainable and Assertive Trade Policy, Brussels, 18.2.2021 COM(2021) 66 final. See also Conclusions of the European Council of 28 June 2018, which invited the European Commission to propose a comprehensive approach to improving, together with like-minded partners, the functioning of the WTO in crucial areas.

First, there are purely economic considerations. The EU is a major trading bloc and the world's largest trader of manufactured goods and services. The EU economy is highly integrated with global value chains and the EU has a number of strategic dependencies. As a result, the EU has a clear interest in shaping the rules applicable to international trade. Given that the EU enjoys trading relations with a large number of partners and has entered into over 70 free trade and other trade and investment agreements, it also has an interest in shaping the rules governing any system for the resolution of disputes.

Second, there are doctrinal reasons. The EU has consistently expressed its commitment to a 'rules-based' trading system built on the principle of multilateralism. This reflects the EU's attachment to the principle of adherence to the rule of law, which is also entrenched within its own legal order. It is identified as a core, constitutional value in Article 2 of the Treaty on European Union, but even before the 'rule of law' had an explicit basis in the treaties, the Court of Justice had established it as a cornerstone of the EU legal order.[83] Other related principles that are also firmly established in EU law are legal certainty and access to justice.[84] Equally, the EU is a multilateral entity itself. Its commitment to finding multilateral solutions to 'common problems' is embedded in Article 20(1) of the Treaty on European Union and remains a political priority,[85] both in its commercial policy and in its broader foreign policy. In a Joint Communication from the Commission and the High Representative, it was reiterated that 'multilateralism has been and will remain the cardinal principle of the EU as the most effective means to govern global relations in a mutually beneficial way'.[86]

Third, there are more pragmatic considerations linked to the dynamics of the current discussions on issues of global concern. The EU has acted as a prime mover, notably in its efforts to regulate, to achieve climate change mitigation, and to address non-trade as well as trade concerns along global value chains. This dynamic approach towards regulation is reflected in new EU instruments such as the carbon border adjustment mechanism (CBAM),[87] and the Deforestation-free

[83] See for instance, Case C-50/00 P, *Unión de Pequeños Agricultores v Council*, ECLI:EU:C:2002:462, paras 38–39; and Case C-402/05 P and C-415/05 P *Kadi and Al Barakaat International Foundation v Council and Commission*, ECLI:EU:C:2008:461, para 316.

[84] For a longer discussion, see P Van Elsuwege and F Gremmelprez, 'Protecting the Rule of Law in the EU Legal Order: A Constitutional Role for the Court of Justice' (2020) 16(1) *European Constitutional Law Review* 8–32.

[85] See for example the 2016 EU Global Strategy.

[86] Joint Communication to the European Parliament and the Council on strengthening the EU's contribution to rules-based multilateralism, JOIN(2021) 3 final.

[87] Regulation of the European Parliament and of the Council establishing a carbon border adjustment mechanism, OJ L 130, 16.5.2023, pp. 52–104.

Products Regulation,[88] both of which have elicited criticism from parts of the WTO membership.[89] The EU has therefore an interest in influencing the ongoing debate as to how to integrate and reconcile trade liberalisation with other core objectives, such as environmental protection and sustainability. Similarly, the EU, as a major donor of development aid across the globe and a core promoter of the Sustainable Development Goals, considers that it has a substantial role in discussions around eligibility for special and differential treatment and how to better integrate developing countries into the WTO system.

A. Asserting Influence in the WTO

It is considerably easier to identify why the EU wishes to exert influence over the different aspects of the WTO reform debate than to ascertain how this may be achieved in practice.

In purely institutional terms, the EU, as one of the 164 members of the WTO, participates in discussions and holds a vote.[90] EU Member States are also independent members of the WTO. Crucially, however, as the majority of issues within the remit of the WTO fall within the scope of Article 207 of the Treaty on Functioning of the European Union (TFEU), they are matters of exclusive Union competence. Consequently, to the extent that the Member States participate in discussions, it is (for the most part) on the basis of a coordinated 'EU' position. In that sense, the EU carries a certain institutional weight as it speaks on behalf of all 27 Member States. Indeed, save in certain areas such as budgetary discussions,[91] it is generally the European Commission (as the external representative of the EU) that takes the lead and intervenes on behalf of the bloc.[92]

This unity of messaging, together with the strength of the European Commission as the primary interlocutor for the EU, is a factor that differentiates the participation of the EU in the WTO as compared to that in some other multilateral fora.[93]

[88] Regulation of the European Parliament and of the Council on the making available on the Union market and the export from the Union of certain commodities and products associated with deforestation and forest degradation and repealing Regulation (EU) No 995/2010, OJ L 150, 9.6.2023, pp 206–47.

[89] See for instance the open letter to the World Trade Organization circulated at the request of the Delegations of Indonesia and Brazil, Letter of 28 November 2022 to the WTO Agricultural Committee, G/AG/GEN/213.

[90] These figures are accurate as of 2022.

[91] Each Member State contributes to the lump sum payable by the EU as its contribution to the WTO.

[92] The EU is represented in the General Council of the WTO by the EU Trade Commissioner.

[93] For instance, the UN where the EU has observer status.

In other words, the EU influence is correlated to its status as a full member, the strength of the competences it enjoys and hence the comparatively limited extent to which it needs to rely on the Member States to represent and express EU interests on its behalf.

In diplomatic, if not in strictly institutional terms, the fact that the EU is a significant economic power undeniably also increases the significance attached by other members to its contributions to reform discussions. It has been argued that both the size of the EU's market and the volume of trade it generates make the EU a key actor in WTO negotiations, and likewise make it improbable that any multilateral agreement could be reached with which it did not agree.[94] This is a point, however, which could be advanced in respect of several other key trading powers. Indeed, the EU itself has identified that convergence with the US is essential, and that the participation of both China and India in the reform process (particularly on market access commitments) is 'indispensable'.[95] Therefore, whilst economic power is certainly a factor which ensures the EU has a loud voice, bridging the 'negotiation gap' with other major economies remains unavoidable to make progress.

In practice, the EU has sought to advance its objectives within the WTO through different mechanisms.

First, the EU has adopted the approach of openly stating a position on issues, formulating this in writing (in the form of position papers or submissions to committees) and circulating this to the membership as a basis for discussion. For instance, the EU has articulated its conception of the priority areas for WTO reform. These were set out in detail in an Annex to the 2021 Trade Policy Review;[96] in February 2023 the EU circulated a communication to the WTO membership on its vision for reform of the WTO Deliberative Function ahead of its submission to the General Council.[97] These positions are also made available in the public domain by the European Commission. This reflects a general approach to transparency[98] around EU objectives and priorities as regards the EU's relationship with

[94] A Dür and H Zimmermann, 'Introduction: The EU in International Trade Negotiations' (2007) 45(4) *Journal of Common Market Studies* 771–87.

[95] Annex to the Communication from the Commission to the European Parliament, the Council, the European Economic and Social Committee and the Committee of the Regions – Trade Policy Review – An Open, Sustainable and Assertive Trade Policy, Brussels, 18.2.2021 COM(2021) 66 final.

[96] ibid.

[97] Reinforcing the Deliberative Function of the WTO to Respond to Global Trade Policy Challenges, Communication from the European Union, 20 February 2023, WT/GC/W/864. Presented to the General Council on 6 March 2023.

[98] A further example is that the EU publishes non-BCI versions (ie not containing business confidential information) of all of its submissions in WTO Dispute Settlement Proceedings.

the WTO that differentiates it from certain other members. China, for instance, rarely sets out its stance in writing.

By formulating and advocating a clear negotiating position, the EU is not only able to share its views across the broader membership, but it also acts as a catalyst for more focused discussions which can coalesce around its proposal. Within the WTO, the issuance of a position paper from one member tends to trigger another member or group of members to respond.[99] Whilst this has been criticised as leading to endless iterations of documents, it nonetheless provides some, meaningful, basis for discussion and forces the membership to focus on specific points.

The EU also participates and makes interventions in the relevant WTO committees. For example, the EU systematically addresses the issue of dispute settlement reform in meetings of the Dispute Settlement Body, where it advocates for the resumption of appointments to the Appellate Body in line with its position that restoration of the two-tier dispute settlement system is a priority.[100] It participates across the spectrum of discussions taking place in the different committees on the various reform agendas. The EU does not, however, generally act as a chairperson, leaving this task to ambassadors from its Member States.

In addition, the EU relies on consensus-building. It has identified that it considers preparatory work with other 'like-minded' WTO members to be crucial to advancing the broader reform agenda. This often takes the form of 'socialising' a text-based proposal in order to garner broader support before formally circulating it to the wider membership. An example of consensus-building occurring in practice is the work on trade and health that was developed through the Ottawa Group[101] in response to the Covid 19 Pandemic. The EU has also fostered further cooperation on addressing climate change and is a co-sponsor of three environmental initiatives: the Trade and Environmental Sustainability Structured Discussions (TESSD), the Informal Dialogue on Plastics Pollution and Sustainable Plastics Trade (IDP), and Fossil Fuel Subsidy Reform (FFSR).

Finally, it is arguably precisely because the EU has a history of engagement with the WTO and its structures that it has acquired credibility in the current discussions around reform.

[99] See, for example, the discussions around special and differential treatment described above.

[100] At the Meeting of the DSB in April 2023, Guatemala, speaking on behalf of 128 Members, introduced for the 65th time the group's proposal to start the selection processes for filling vacancies on the Appellate Body. The EU took the floor in support of the Appellate Body nominations.

[101] The Ottawa Group comprises the EU and 13 other like-minded members. In June 2022 it also issued a Joint Statement on WTO reform.

B. Measuring the Influence of the EU in the WTO Reform Process

It is notoriously difficult to measure the influence of any one participant in a multilateral negotiation. Indeed, as regards the influence of the EU as a global actor more generally, it has been questioned how 'external impact' can be defined and measured at all.[102] If the benchmark is linked to the EU's stated, initial objectives true 'influence' arguably depends on the degree of ambition. In the context of the WTO reform process and given the decision-making processes within the WTO which are consensus-based, this is inextricably linked to the extent to which the EU position is aligned with the views of the wider membership. That is a variable metric depending on the precise item on the WTO reform agenda.

As described above, the EU has transparently articulated its negotiating stance in respect of several of the core pillars of potential WTO reform, including the deliberative function and the proposals for reform of the dispute settlement mechanism.[103] The extent to which EU objectives are reflected in the negotiated outcomes will, therefore, be one means of determining the EU's contribution to any reform *post hoc*. Assessing how and to what extent the EU is influencing the WTO reform process whilst it is underway is a more complex task.

To an extent, the role any member is playing within the WTO discussions is self-proclamatory. Yet it is possible for one member to take a lead in a particular discussion. A recent example is the role played by India in securing the Agreement on Fisheries Subsidies. That India had played a central role in brokering the final agreement is undoubtedly correct; the magnitude of that role is harder to evaluate from an external perspective. In any event, following the negotiations, the Indian Commerce and Industry Minister, Piyush Goyal told the awaiting press that India had turned the tide of negotiations from 'failure, gloom and doom to optimism, enthusiasm and consensus-based decision-making'.[104] Similarly, the EU's statements characterising itself as a 'leading player' in the on-going reform debate is not without foundation, even if its significance remains difficult to quantify precisely.

[102] M Carbone, 'Making a difference in multilateral negotiations: the European Union and the global agenda on aid effectiveness' (2021) 7(4) *Global Affairs* 453–70.
[103] See also European Commission, 'WTO modernisation. Introduction to future EU proposals' (18 September 2018), available on the website of the Directorate General for Trade: The EU and the WTO (europa.eu).
[104] 'India turned the tide of negotiations from failure to optimism: Piyush Goyal after WTO meeting' – ThePrint – ANIFeed, 17 June 2022.

There is one respect in which the EU has had a tangible influence. This is in addressing the 'void' left by the Appellate Body crisis. The EU played a major part in establishing, together with 20 other members, the Multi-Party Interim Appeal Arbitration Arrangement (MPIA).

Article 25 of the Dispute Settlement Understanding (DSU) provides that arbitration may be used as an alternative method of dispute settlement to standard WTO Panel and Appellate Body proceedings. Under the MPIA, adherents agree to submit to binding arbitration to resolve any appeal in relation to future disputes. Annex 1 to the MPIA sets out a template of rules designed to govern that arbitration. To the extent that those rules are silent on a specific procedural question, they include a *renvoi* to the provisions of the DSU and other rules and procedures applicable to Appellate Review.[105] This temporary arrangement is designed to offer a means to secure two-tier dispute resolution in the absence of a functioning Appellate Body, whilst retaining a link to the core principles of the DSU and the WTO Agreements.

The EU has undoubtedly helped to secure the success of the MPIA. First, the EU was instrumental in the design and establishment of the system set up under the MPIA. Second, the EU has worked with partners to ensure an increasing 'buy-in' to this mechanism. Third, the EU has itself used the system it helped to create: the first appeal to be heard by the MPIA towards the end of 2022 was in a dispute brought by the EU against Colombia.[106]

There are members who remain sceptical about this alternative dispute resolution system. Since the establishment of the MPIA, both the US and Indonesia have eschewed this option (neither are parties to the MPIA) and have appealed unfavourable Panel reports 'into the void'. As explained above, this has the effect of preventing their formal adoption by the Dispute Settlement Body. Until such time as any appeal is heard, those members are not bound to bring the disputed measures into compliance.

Admittedly, it is less obvious whether the EU will succeed in securing its objectives as regards restoring the Appellate Body. Nevertheless, it is arguably in helping shape solutions, albeit ones that are supposed to be temporary, that the EU's influence could have the furthest reach: first, in terms of leading by example – most clearly evidenced by using the MPIA procedures to resolve a

[105] Paragraph 11 of Annex 1 specifies that MPIA arbitrations 'shall be governed, *mutatis mutandis*, by the provisions of the DSU and other rules and procedures applicable to Appellate Review', https://docs.wto.org/dol2fe/Pages/FE_Search/FE_S_S009-DP.aspx?language=E&CatalogueIdList=263504.

[106] DS591: *Colombia – Frozen Fries*. Colombia appealed the Panel Report.

dispute; second, in showing flexibility to adapt and apply modified procedural rules, albeit that the rules of the MPIA are anchored in the existing legal framework under the DSU.[107]

IV. Conclusion

The WTO has struggled to adapt to a rapidly changing geopolitical context and to secure agreements amongst its diverse membership. It has to grapple with a panoply of reform agenda items which relate not only to the core of its activities, but also to the procedures and structures which govern it. To remain relevant as an actor in the global governance of international trade, reform is now both inevitable and urgent.

Given the diverse drivers for change, together with the interlinkages between them, one of the many challenges in this process will be setting the priorities for a membership with diverging economic interests. The EU, with its clear strategic interest and dependency on international trade, has vocalised its policy objective of playing a prominent role in shaping the future of the WTO. As a *sui generis* international organisation itself, the EU has also been confronted with the need to address and adapt to global challenges that are fundamentally different from those that existed at the time it was created. In that sense, it is arguably uniquely placed to assist in the process of reform.

The extent to which the EU will be able to influence the outcomes of WTO reform in the face of an increasingly polarised membership remains unclear. Increasingly, the EU, like other members, is pursuing bilateral solutions in parallel with multilateral discussions. A key question for the future is whether this growing network of bilateral arrangements will help to build consensus to achieve meaningful reform within the WTO, or rather accelerate its demise.

[107] For an analysis of the MPIA see B McGarry and N Zargarinejad, 'Tracing the Powers of WTO MPIA Arbitrators' (2022–2023) 8(2) *McGill Journal of Dispute Resolution* 1–22.

8

On the importance of attributes to the imperative

Objectives are defined by the attributes of the entities involved.

This statement is objective, global and universal.

HERMES.— I agree with you. Now, going back to our leg hair removal scenario, why did we reach differing conclusions when we said that feeling attractive was the objective, and when we had no objective at all?

XARGOS.— This is a subtlety that eludes me. Something tells me that having an objective meant we didn't have to completely undo each and every change produced by the action. According to your earlier reasoning, the natural order makes it possible to undo globally. Having an objective allows us to undo only the effects on the objects directly involved.

HERMES.— That's right. When we perform an action, we go from an initial situation to a final situation. Between these two, certain objects are acted upon. As a result of that action, they undergo changes to certain of their attributes.

XARGOS.— What are those?

HERMES.— Attributes are qualities or properties. Qualities, in turn, are the characteristics, whether natural or acquired, that distinguish people, living beings in general, and things. A quality is also the way of being of a person or thing. Property refers to the right or faculty to possess something, and be able to dispose of it within legal limits. A right, in turn, is a human being's natural faculty to legitimately pursue his or her purposes in life, but it also means the faculty to do or demand everything that the laws or authorities establish in our favour, or that the owner of an object allows us to do with it. A faculty is the same thing as an aptitude, which is the quality that makes an object apt, adequate, or accommodating of a particular purpose. It's also the sufficiency or suitability for obtaining and exercising a job or post, and the capacity or willingness to perform well in a business, industry, art, or other field.

XARGOS.— So, when any of the things you just mentioned is modified, we are modifying an attribute.

HERMES.— Yes. Some of the attributes we could mention are colour, shape, personality, and existence.

XARGOS.— Right now I can't remember why it's so important for us to know what attributes are. What could they mean for our purposes? We were just wondering why to include objectives in the criterion we're creating. That's all.

HERMES.— They're important because they are what change when an action is performed on an object. The object changes because its attributes do, or vice-versa. If we consider performing an action without objective, the opposite action would be the one that returns all attributes of all relevant objects to their initial state. As we said several times, this is impossible. However, when we have an objective, the opposite action only has to undo the changes made to certain attributes.

XARGOS.— Why?

HERMES.— Because those are the attributes that must change in order to meet the objective. Let's say that the attributes that interest us are those that define the object. The other changes that could occur are unimportant for achieving our purpose. The undo action is the opposite of the first action because when it's performed, it leaves the objective unmet once again, not because it returns each and every attribute to its original state.

XARGOS.— Like you said, it seems logical that the important attributes are those used to define the objective. But perhaps they're not the only ones. Maybe they are, or maybe they're not. How shall we find them?

HERMES.— Let's find them together, but they should certainly have some kind of direct relationship to the objective considered. After all, the objective made it possible to reduce all the attributes to just a few.

XARGOS.— That certainly is the only way I can think of to start.

HERMES.— The leg hair removal scenario helped us realise the importance of the objective. It also warned us of the problems that arise when the interests of two beings are mixed, and therefore of the need for dialogue. Right now we're not interested in reasoning about whether we're acting against the interests of the body. Besides, I'm getting tired of that scenario. So, shall we find another example to solve the problem of attributes?

XARGOS.— OK. We could imagine a person who wants to keep their home warm in the winter in order to be happy.

HERMES.— That seems as good as any other example involving no more than one being with the ability to create order, and it helps us focus on the problem of attributes. This person's objective is to be warm inside the house, and they assess all the actions within their reach to achieve this. They can install and turn on a heating system powered by electricity, gas, wood, etc. They conclude that since they live in a forest, a wood-burning system requires less effort. They imagine the action already completed, and find that the action has affected the following objects: the house, firewood, and fireplace. Some attributes of these objects change as a result of the action. In their initial state, we have a cold house, unused firewood, and a clean fireplace. In their final state, we have a warm house, burnt firewood, and a dirty fireplace. Have I forgotten any objects or attributes?

XARGOS.— I don't think so. Go on.

HERMES.— This person must now establish the opposite action that would return all the objects to their initial state. However, we know that if we try to undo the effects on all the attributes, the opposite action is impossible. In this example, it's easy to visualise because it's impossible to restore the 'un-burnt' attribute to the burnt firewood.

XARGOS.— And going back to the subject of leg hair removal without an objective, in that case it was impossible to restore the waxed hairs to their un-waxed state.

HERMES.— Yes. But Xargos, you seem a bit obsessed with the leg hair removal scenario, and I already told you that was a dangerous subject!

XARGOS.— Hermes, don't make me laugh. This is a serious business!

HERMES.— OK. You're also right about the leg hair. As we've seen, opposite actions need only restore the attributes of objects that truly reflect the desired good in the objective. In the hair removal scenario, the desired good affected the body, which had to be attractive. All that was required for it to become less attractive was the passage of time. Whatever happened to the leg hair once it was removed was irrelevant. In our last example, the objective was to keep the house warm. The object affected by the opposite action was the house, and the attribute to be restored was the heat, which had to dissipate and let the cold return. In this case, the opposite action that would make the warm house cold would be to simply put out the fire and wait. This would require much less effort than adding firewood to the hearth, after first gathering the wood. We would therefore conclude that we should perform the action; we should heat the house.

XARGOS.— I'm having more and more fun, and the criterion is starting to feel like a hobby. Now that our ideas are getting clearer, shall we go back and analyse the objects and attributes in the first three examples we discussed: the builder, the destroyer of sheds, and the student?

HERMES.— Well, the builder's objective was to protect his tools. The action was to build a shed using the tools. The objects involved in the action were the tools, construction materials, and the shed. The initial state was characterised by the following attributes: unused tools, unused construction materials, and an unbuilt shed. The objects and attributes in their final state were used tools, used materials, and a built shed. The good produced by achieving the objective is the completed shed, so the opposite action would have to affect the shed. It would turn the built shed into a non-existent shed. In other words, it could be any destructive action we can think of. You go ahead and do the other two cases.

XARGOS.— Right. The destroyer of sheds' objective would be to tear down the shed for fun. The action is to demolish the shed using the tools stored inside. The objects involved are the destroyer, the tools, and the shed. The initial state is characterised by a rested destroyer, unused tools, and the shed in good condition. The final state is characterised by a tired destroyer, used tools, and a ruined shed. Again, the object involved in the objective is the shed. The opposite action must affect the shed, and should turn the ruined shed into one in good condition. In other words, if it was completely destroyed, the opposite action would be to build another shed.

HERMES.— I agree. And you were right to include the destroyer of sheds among the objects involved. I forgot to include the builder in my example.

XARGOS.— The student's objective was to learn because he thought that would bring him closer to happiness. The actions for achieving this objective were to go to school and study. The objects involved are the student, school materials, books, school, and teachers. The initial state is characterised by a student without knowledge, unused materials, unused books, an unused school, and rested teachers. The final state is characterised by a knowledgeable student, used materials, used books, and a school and teachers that have suffered some wear and tear. The object involved in the objective is the student, and the undo action should affect him by taking him from a situation where he has knowledge to a situation where he doesn't. The action requiring the least effort to achieve this objective is to quit studying and let time pass.

HERMES.— That's right. And since doing nothing requires zero effort, and studying does require an effort even if done as efficiently as possible, he should conclude that he has to study. And he would reach this conclusion even if no one explained this to him.

XARGOS.— It took us a long time to get this far, but now everything's starting to make sense.

HERMES.— We've definitely learned a lot about the criterion we discussed, and I think it's time to restructure it with the new considerations we've added. Let's establish the action criterion as follows. First, the objective pursued must be clearly proposed. If it's a direct action, we must identify the objective pursued based on that action. Second, we have to investigate whether our objective is intermingled with the interests of other beings consciously or unconsciously endowed with the ability to act. If such beings exist, we start a dialogue with them to establish a common objective satisfactory to everyone. Third, once the objective has been established, we list all possible actions that could achieve it. Fourth, we choose the least costly action for achieving the objective. Fifth, we establish the objects affected by the action, and verify which attributes would be changed by performing the action. Sixth, of all the actions listed, we choose the one directly affecting whether the good defined by the objective is met, and the attributes that ensure the objective will be achieved. Seventh, we establish the opposite action or actions that would return those attributes of the selected object to their initial state. We consider whether the actions interfere with anyone's objectives and, if so, we establish those actions in a dialogue common to everyone. Ninth, we list all actions that would achieve this new objective, which is to return the relevant attributes of that object to their initial state, and choose the least costly action on the list. Tenth, we compare the two most efficient actions selected, and choose the costlier of the two. This way, we would know which action to choose; in other words, we would know how to act.

XARGOS.— Knowing that we should only act when we have an objective, that to be happy we must not be passive, and that both of these conclusions were reached by applying our criterion as you described it, I think you just summarised it perfectly. And since the objective must be known in order to act, and we have to reason to know our objective, irrational impulsive people have cause to fear. When they act, and act again to fix what they've ruined without really knowing what they're doing, they only disorder the Universe, their environment, and generate unhappiness. Or perhaps we rational people should be fearful of their presence?

HERMES.— I think you just discovered a clear split in the union we were seeking. On one side we have rational people, and on the other the 'irrationals'.

9

On whether the imperative leads to forgiveness and self-improvement. The need for education and social structures

Study, education and the professions are necessary to ensure that dialogue generates consensus, and therefore objectives.

This statement is objective, global and universal.

XARGOS.— From everything we've said, the only explanations I can think of for people to behave irrationally is that their common sense fails them, they are unaware of or have no knowledge of their environment, or they are ill and unable to face the situation.

HERMES.— I find that statement to be quite harsh. However, you just might be right. To minimise this problem, a basic requirement would be a good education that manages to convey the obvious, the existence of the natural order. Common sense would confirm the truth of such teaching. The rest, through appropriately guided learning, would naturally emerge in the students.

HERMES.— Right now, I think we're very close to achieving our stated objective. Imagine that humankind has consciously absorbed, through each and every one of its individuals, the observations we've made tonight. Once this understanding is acquired, no one will doubt its truthfulness because the common sense gained through experience supports it. Society would have to move rapidly. Perhaps an even faster development than we've seen in the technological sector. The result would be equally spectacular. Each individual would start out with identical knowledge of the natural order, and the search for happiness would proceed based on the greatest possible and appropriate order. Each individual would also have an objective method for assessing their actions and deciding when their actions are right or wrong. Finally, each individual would identify the natural order as the possible cause of their unhappiness, and would know that this should be the focus of all their actions. In this humankind of the future we are positing, wouldn't feelings of powerlessness caused by frustration be overcome? And wouldn't the condemnation of others disappear?

XARGOS.— You'll have to explain that to me, but I think you're moving into the field of sociology or psychology, where we're not experts.

HERMES.— It's true that we might touch on those fields, but I don't think we'd be making a serious error by discussing from an inexpert perspective what we think might happen. At this point, I also think it's our obligation to take a risk. If we conclude that the result of our approach is disastrous, or different for each individual, we certainly won't have achieved the objective we established when we began our dialogue.

XARGOS.— Let's proceed then, but I'd like us to be prudent. Let's try to say as little as possible on this subject.

HERMES.— I can explain more clearly with an example. I was saying that the feeling of powerlessness and condemnatory judgments against third parties would tend to disappear, and that notions of self-improvement and forgiveness would appear in their place. Each and every individual would continuously seek to perform those acts that increase order for any of the objects they act upon. They'd know that when they perform an action, they will have to put in more effort, because they're fighting against the natural order to achieve their objective. It's no surprise, when the adversary is so great, that a multitude of actions fail, resulting in frustration. Such frustration can produce a feeling of powerlessness, demoralizing the individual, resulting in a sense of unease in the way of happiness. But with our way of thinking, the individual wouldn't have the chance to feel this unease. They would instead recall the greatness of the enemy: the natural order itself. The conclusion is simple: it's normal for some of the actions we attempt to end in failure because the undertaking is so daring. We must therefore seek new mechanisms to prevent failure. As we seek to better ourselves, we must increase our effort, so that our actions don't fail. Similarly, we're likely to see third parties fail in their own attempts to increase order. Such people should not be judged as incompetent, but treated with the understanding they deserve. They too are attempting to fight against that enemy we call the natural order. Feelings of forgiveness should emerge naturally. We must forgive and help in every way we can. That way, on the next attempt, they might manage to improve their tactic against the common enemy.

XARGOS.— I don't dare say you're right, although it certainly appears that what you describe should result from the principles we've established.

HERMES.— To give you an example, we could imagine a sick person who, for lack of knowledge, is unable to restore the lost order in his body, and therefore goes to a doctor. If humankind were as we imagine it, the doctor should treat the patient with understanding because he knows that the illness is caused solely by the natural order, not by the patient. The patient should also treat the doctor with understanding because the doctor is involved in a great undertaking against the natural order, which is much stronger than any physician. If the result of the treatment is satisfactory, they should both be glad, and the doctor should be congratulated for achieving something almost impossible: re-establishing order where the natural order had imposed disorder. If the treatment were not satisfactory, the patient should forgive the doctor because, in spite of all his or her efforts to re-establish order, the natural order was not defeated. A doctor who has clearly fought as hard as possible should be congratulated. In turn, the physician should not feel powerless. Rather, the frustration resulting from that attempt should help him or her gain sufficient strength for self-improvement towards acquiring the knowledge necessary to not fail in the next case. Tutors and professors also struggle to instil an appropriate order in the minds of their students. Their enemy, the natural order, will try to prevent this, so it makes sense that they'll sometimes fail in the attempt and despair. Shouldn't we be understanding, and provide them with the necessary resources so that the undesirable result does not recur?

XARGOS.— The situation you describe is truly beautiful, but far removed from today's reality. For example, doctors are quickly condemned even when they've fought as hard as possible against an illness. The patient immediately blames the doctor, who protects himself by affecting a distant manner with the patient. From the beginning, the patient suffers from a feeling of insecurity and lack of trust in his physician, and ends up complaining of a lack of professionalism. This vicious circle can quickly lead to a lack of humility on both sides, and a clear alienation.

HERMES.— Yes, the current situation is far removed from the humankind we were imagining, and not only from the patient's perspective. We could also talk about negligence from people performing shoddy work, who seek only easy money. There are examples in the medical profession, but also in every sector of society. The finance industry, for example. According to our discussion tonight, the main cause of these confrontations is the fact that human beings have not accepted the natural order as it is. The enemy tends to eliminate everything that causes happiness, and give us those things that cause unhappiness. This means that the pursuit of happiness is associated with a certain amount of effort, and even so is not always possible to achieve. If we also act unconsciously, unaware of the scope of the decisions we make, we'll probably only accelerate the natural process of destroying order.

XARGOS.— Now I remember an issue that we have left unsolved.

HERMES.— What is that?

XARGOS.— We said that the existence of evil people could mean that the unification of all human beings will be impossible.

HERMES.— You're right, we left that discussion for the end of our dialogue, and I agree that the time is coming. I understand *evil person* to be someone who chooses to harm other people or themselves in order to achieve their own purpose. In other words, someone who follows some type of ideal contrary to the interests of humankind. Do you agree?

XARGOS.— Yes, that's what I was referring to.

HERMES.— It's obvious that to go against humankind, they won't engage in a dialogue with other people. If they did seek common objectives, they would never become harmful. It's easy to find an endless source of examples simply by looking at those people who refuse to engage in dialogue. However, the same is true of people who don't apply an action criterion that ensures minimum disorder even when they do participate in a dialogue. For example, there are people whose mission is to make the dialogue never-ending in order to gain time and maximise their personal benefit, who will do so even knowing that their personal benefit will result in a high social cost. Others will use their knowledge of their opponents' ethical framework and moral criteria to anticipate their actions. This category could include all ideologies that lead to situations of aggression against third parties, such as dictatorships, terrorism, vandalism, organised crime, and even religious sects. On this occasion, I think we're very close to a solution. We recognised that the natural order tends to seek disorder in all sensory objects to which it has access. A human being is a sensory object to which the natural order has access. It's possible for some human beings to lose their mental order, and seek only their own benefit rather than that of humankind. Although humans have the ability to create order, they also have the ability to create disorder. Those unfortunate people may choose not to follow the criterion established here, and not always seek the greatest amount of order possible for all humankind, and thus become its enemies.

XARGOS.— But if they were taught how the natural order works, they would have to stop behaving that way. In other words, if there were adequate education...

HERMES.— Yes, many would abandon such disastrous behaviour, but others would be swept away by the natural order. Unfortunately, the natural order itself makes sure that there are always individuals with these characteristics, which means that human beings have to establish organisations responsible for keeping such individuals under control. We can therefore conclude that we'll always need judicial, legislative, and executive powers, for example. Democracy must continue to act as an inevitable framework that allows humankind to exercise its freedom and protect itself from individuals whose objective is no longer the good of humankind. Those who pursue their own benefit at the expense of others. Luckily, some of these people are only bad due to ignorance, and some will be reconverted through education. The only people left on the side of crime would be those who are truly ill, having been disordered by the natural order. Humankind must protect itself from these individuals through mechanisms obtained in accordance with the criterion we established, and must treat these people with the compassion they deserve. These protective mechanisms must at least include dialogue with all persons involved.

XARGOS.— I don't know if we're behaving like politicians. This may be the part of our dialogue that I've liked the least, because I would wish for the existence of a completely happy world. But it seems obvious that if we accept the existence of the natural order, as our common sense tells us to, there must be disorder in all sensory objects, including human intellect. Therefore, there will always be a certain number of people who behave in a disordered manner. Luckily, the number of individuals in that group will be very small in comparison to the multitude, so the continuity of a new, united humankind remains assured.

HERMES.— That would be fortunate. It's part of humankind's duty to keep the number of such individuals to a minimum. Let's verify this, and imagine that humankind is considering whether or not this is its duty. In other words, the objective is to ensure that no harmful individuals exist. After consideration it is determined that education, integration, and healthcare, activities requiring great effort, are nevertheless the most efficient way of achieving this. To undo the effects, humankind would simply have to let its individuals become ill, uneducated, and not integrated. There would now be individuals who are harmful, who were harmless before. This all requires zero effort. The first action would have to be chosen as the correct option. This confirms that part of humankind's duty does indeed lie here.

XARGOS.— Quite a while ago, you promised a link independent of each person's beliefs. You also said that if we didn't find it, there would be no such universal link. Well, the time has come: The very rule we created predicts the existence of differences. Even if detestable behaviours, even if few in number, they nevertheless exist. There will always be people who don't agree with this rule, who produce harm and unhappiness.

HERMES.— That's true. However, these detestable behaviours, as you described them, were excluded. All others remain intact and protected by the umbrella of our reasoning.

XARGOS.— Are you assuring me that all other beliefs, including religions, that we might describe as good, are protected by the rule of action we deduced?

HERMES.— Yes, that's the way it should be. After all, we've created a criterion that selects the things we would describe as good, which are those that lead to happiness.

XARGOS.— And those who don't follow the criterion are therefore unobservant or ill. I still find it rather harsh.

HERMES.— So do I, but we already said that the unobservant would convert voluntarily through education. We might describe them as *morally ill*. We're all unobservant when something doesn't concern us, unless someone tells us where to look. So, the only ones left would be the second group, whose numbers we can expect to be low. If society also protects itself adequately and treats them as people who are ill, we will have achieved the best of cultures.

XARGOS.— What you're describing is not very different from what's already being done in a very localised manner. Dialogue has led to democracy, and within democracy, to education, protective institutions, and assistance for the ill.

HERMES.— Humans had to make progress in some area these past two thousand, five hundred years. And we'd still have to see whether they're doing it by indiscriminately disordering more than they're ordering, and whether they are, in fact, efficient. What makes us different from the ideal society we discussed is that up to now, we were lacking the criterion to stabilise the situation as the optimum available.

XARGOS.— You've got too much faith in that criterion we just brought into being. And to top it off, common sense predicts what we all already know, that there will always be people who make our lives miserable for their own benefit. Even though you described them as ill, they'll still be there.

10

On whether to listen to one's heart or to reason

Reason is necessary for defining objectives.

This statement is objective, global and universal.

After these last words were spoken, Hermes listened quietly to the sounds of the night, including soft breathing from Xargos, who was lying some distance away. It was still a peaceful night, but the temperature had dropped during the course of their conversation. The cold and wind, along with the memory of those last words spoken, gave Hermes goose bumps. Finally, after being momentarily chilled by the wind, he relaxed and gazed at the sky, which was still full of stars. He had no way of knowing whether Xargos felt the same restlessness, but it was easy to imagine that he did.

Everything they had said and reasoned now seemed frivolous and lacking in consistency. Inside, he wished for the world to be perfect, for all this to be a dream where it doesn't matter what is thought or said, where we're safe because a higher God is protecting us. But his reason leaned toward acknowledging the reality of the natural order through common sense. In this case, his heart and his reason did not seem to understand each other. It occurred to Hermes, as a game, to put everything they'd discussed that night to the test on this specific problem: What should I do? Do I listen to my heart, or to reason?

If I listen to my heart, I shouldn't worry about what happens. Once in that state of lost responsibility, how could I return to the situation where I am now? Should I forget that state of irresponsibility, and accept the risk of making a mistake on my own? Of the two paths, the second one seems more tiring than the first. So, according to our reasoning, I shouldn't follow my heart.

If I listen to reason every time I make a decision, I'll have to make sure it's the correct one. Each decision will require me to make a comparison between performing each action and not doing so. That would require an effort I wouldn't have to make if I go back to the situation promoted by my heart. It seems that the option I should choose is to follow reason.

Because the heart contains all our impulsive, irrational, unthinking and intuitive tendencies, and also reflects that need for a father figure who would assume responsibility for our actions, deciding not to listen to one's heart tends to minimise all those impulses. This is the result of our reflection.

I guess now is when I would pray to God to give us enough strength to successfully conclude the task of listening to reason, and thereby achieve the greatest amount of order possible.

This does not seem to be an easy task. If I were religious, and now I understand why religion is accepted, I would simply have to follow the norms of my religion as they've been established, and commend all my actions to its care. In a way, I would wash my hands of part of my responsibility. But this normative rigidity, that would relieve me of part of my responsibility, loses the objectivity it needs to be universal. It's true that less responsibility also translates into reduced personal effort during correct decision-making: many decisions become immediate or unquestionable. But whether or not the decision is correct is restricted to a prior covenant established by the religion.

As a selfish person, I'd be interested in a religion whose maturity relieved me of the burden of constantly being the guardian of my own decisions. Each human being can choose the spiritual guide that facilitates this journey to a greater extent. However, on this path, conflict is guaranteed.

Just as there are different types of screwdrivers depending on the screws being used, it's completely logical for religion to become a tool that will adopt different forms to ensure its effectiveness for a particular person. It's useless to try to force a star head screw using a flat screwdriver, just because flat screwdrivers work wonderfully well with slotted screws. Forcefully imposing the use of flat screwdrivers on all types of screw heads might end up being an effective solution, but it certainly wouldn't be efficient. It seems more logical to let each screw try to find the screwdriver designed for it, if screws were capable of intelligence and free choice.

We could say that the existence of God and an accompanying religion could generate a tool that, if tuned finely enough, could help us successfully achieve our daily personal objective of striving to increase the order that leads to happiness. However, it would not be universal.

Hermes had been pondering these problems for quite a while, and all he could glimpse was the tip of the iceberg. Everything seemed to indicate that the problems considered had been discussed superficially, leaving plenty more to talk about. However, something inside said they were not far from the truth. Maybe they hadn't gone about it in the best way, hadn't reasoned far enough, or perhaps there were counterexamples that would refute what they'd said about the natural order, for example. Even so, he knew they were getting close to something truly important.

The sound of light footsteps in the underbrush distracted Hermes from his thoughts. He opened his eyes and discovered again how beautiful the night was. There, in the middle of the countryside, surrounded by darkness, he could feel like a citizen of the world. Place was the least important thing. He could be in his native village, or in any other. He understood that wherever each human being went, they would have exactly the same concerns. The only difference might be that he wouldn't have devoted time to considering such questions. An even closer sound took him back to the magic of that night.

A beautiful young woman appeared out of nowhere. Her body was perfect, and her figure was enhanced by the close-fitting clothes she undoubtedly liked to wear. She exuded the freshness of freedom. Her face combined serenity with confidence, making her extremely attractive. You might say she was nearly irresistible.

'Hi. Who are you?' asked Hermes, almost without thinking.

11

The universal categorical imperative

There is a universal categorical imperative.

This statement is objective, global and universal.

STRANGER.— My name is Mara. I've been listening to *human* voices in the distance for a while, and curiosity has brought me to this place. I thought you might be telling scary stories because I'm sure I didn't hear laughter. In fact, I'm almost convinced that they were horror stories because at some point the breeze brought the words *leg hair removal* to my ears.

XARGOS.— If you'd like to join our discussion, you're very welcome. Our names are Hermes and Xargos. With us around, it's hardly surprising that the breeze startled you with that sort of vocabulary. We weren't telling scary stories; we were just spending this night trying to discover whether humankind could ever unite independently of its religion, politics, nationality, race, or anything else.

MARA.— A difficult task, but you've been talking for so long without raising your voices that I'd say you've gone far, and in common agreement.

HERMES.— Well, that does seem to be the case this time. If you'd like to join us, we can give you a summary of the main conclusions we've reached.

MARA.— I'd love that.

XARGOS.— Hermes, if you don't mind, let me be the one to do the summary. I'd like to make sure I remember each and every one of the important parts. If you don't agree with something, you can stop me.

HERMES.— No problem.

XARGOS.— Right, here comes the summary. First, we established that the natural order consists of the tendency of all sensory objects to move toward disorder. We said that breaking down, deteriorating, and becoming ill are all different manifestations of disorder. The natural order can necessarily be deduced through each human being's common sense, and will therefore become the heritage of humankind once consciously assimilated by everyone. We defined the happiness of human beings as the state of mind that delights in obtaining certain goods favourable to it. Similarly, unhappiness is associated with the loss of such goods. We suggested that all goods favourable to human beings for achieving happiness are associated with an order that the natural order itself tends to destroy. This showed us that a man, if he's unable to act appropriately, quickly loses the goods he possesses and enters into a state of unhappiness. To prevent this from happening, he must struggle against the natural order, creating and maintaining order wherever disorder would naturally take its place. Struggling against the natural order takes effort. The existence of this effort helped us find a criterion, which we believe is quite universal, for distinguishing right from wrong, or the goods and actions that produce happiness from those that do not. This action criterion involves first reasoning as follows, before performing any action. First, we evaluate the objective to be achieved with the action. Second, we seek all possible actions that are different from the first, but would achieve the same objective. Third, of all those actions, we identify the one requiring the least effort, and choose that as the most efficient option, and therefore the best. Fourth, we identify the objects, and the attributes of those objects, affected by the action, and select the ones directly included in the definition of the objective. Fifth, we identify all possible opposite actions that could be performed after the action in question to restore the initial attributes of the selected objects, and therefore leave the proposed objective unmet. Sixth, we choose the most efficient of those actions. Seventh, we compare the effort required to perform the action and the opposite action. If the effort required to perform the action in the most efficient manner exceeds the effort required to perform the opposite action in the most efficient manner, we should perform the action. Otherwise, we should not perform any action. Throughout this process, we have to be careful and check whether our objective is interrelated to those of other beings. If so, we should establish our objectives and actions by common agreement through dialogue. Applying the criterion to two general cases led us to deduce that we should not act for the sake of acting, and we should not be passive; otherwise, we'll move away from happiness. After this, we entered into discussions that showed that the natural order itself would ensure a minimum number of individuals within humankind who would not accept this way of thinking, mainly due to their inability to find such order while struggling against the disorder that seeks to overcome them. This last reflection showed us the need for an adequate model of government to protect humankind from these individuals, who must be considered ill, and therefore treated to the maximum extent possible. If there were people who were not guided this way, and were not ill, it would be due to a deficiency in the educational system.

MARA.— Wow! I think I like this way of thinking because, for the first time, I can make sense of the cardinal virtues. Is this reasoning your own, or did you read about it somewhere?

XARGOS.— I don't usually read about this sort of thing, but from now on I'm going to try.

HERMES.— We structured it tonight while we were talking, and I'm really surprised we've taken it so far. I don't think it's our own reasoning now, but one belonging to humankind. I'm sure any other two human beings in the mood for a night of dialogue could have come up with this way of thinking. But Mara, why did you say you can make sense of the cardinal virtues now?

12

On whether the universal categorical imperative makes the people using it virtuous

The universal categorical imperative leads to the cardinal virtues. This statement is objective, global and universal.

MARA.— The cardinal virtues have fascinated me since I was a little girl. At school, I remember how an individual possessing them was described as virtuous. To refresh our memory, the cardinal virtues are prudence, justice, fortitude, and temperance. It was always said that to abide by the Lord's wishes, and be at peace with oneself and others, we must not abandon the path of righteousness. When we asked what the path of righteousness was, we were told that it was the path of virtue. This type of answer always surprised me because if you inquired a bit further, you'd conclude that being virtuous was more or less the same as being prudent, just, temperate, and possessing fortitude at the same time. When I was still a little girl, and determined not to be discouraged, I decided to investigate the meaning of each of these words containing virtue. I discovered that prudence was the ability to discern and distinguish right from wrong, in order to pursue it or avoid it. I did the same thing with temperance, and found that it means moderating one's appetites and the excessive use of the senses by subjecting them to reason. I discovered that fortitude means defeating fear and fleeing from temerity, and that justice is the virtue that leans toward giving each party that which corresponds to or belongs to them. So, in response to the question 'How can I act righteously?', I now had four questions: How can I distinguish right from wrong? How can I moderate my appetites and the excessive use of my senses? How can I defeat fear and flee from temerity? How can I know what belongs to whom? The situation was starting to get terribly complicated. At this rate, I would soon abandon my efforts. To be virtuous, you would have to at least read every treatise ever written on philosophy, theology, and law. Virtue seemed inaccessible to a simple human being like me, who was not a scholar in those areas. And now that I've adopted a pessimistic tone, why not add these other questions to the four I mentioned above: What is right? What is wrong? What are appetites? When is a sense used excessively? What is temerity? We could now continue by defining temerity, for example, and discover that it involves excessively imprudent actions when confronting dangers, or actions that are said, done, or thought without any grounds, reason, or motive. I'm sure we now have more questions. The path seems infinitely long and difficult. However, your approach opens my eyes again, and invites me to gather my strength. It seems like a much more certain process.

HERMES.— You'll probably think I'm trying to chat you up, but I'm truly impressed by what you just said. Really! It's not empty praise, just reality.

XARGOS.—You should proceed a bit more virtuously, for example, by showing a bit of temperance so you don't make our unknown speaker uncomfortable. By the way, she's doing a great job.

MARA.— Thanks for the compliments, guys, but right now I prefer philosophical discussions to having to choose between the two of you.

HERMES.— Don't worry, that was just a quick breather. I really needed it so I could follow you properly. I'm dying to hear your conclusion.

XARGOS.— I'm with Hermes! I can't wait to hear more.

MARA.— Well, I think the conclusion is simple. Prudence, as we said, means being able to discern and distinguish right from wrong, in order to follow or avoid it. Doesn't your action criterion enable you to make precisely that distinction?

HERMES.— I think so.

MARA.— Well, that means there's no doubt that anyone who applies your way of reasoning to discern the actions or goods that lead to good things, will be prudent.

HERMES.— It seems like they must be.

MARA.— Temperance means moderating your appetites and the excessive use of the senses by subjecting them to reason. From what I can see, temperance is precisely the virtue that involves applying prudence to one's appetites and senses. Imagine that we're faced with an insatiable appetite. Before letting ourselves get swept away, reason considers whether or not to allow this, in accordance with your prudence criterion. Reason would establish satisfying the appetite as the objective. It would later seek the different actions that could be taken to satisfy that appetite. Of all those actions, it would choose the one requiring the least effort. It would later establish undoing the previous action as the objective; in other words, going back to leaving the appetite unsatisfied, like it was at the beginning. It would discover that this objective is impossible to achieve; in other words, we are not capable of performing that action. It would therefore conclude that the effort required is beyond human capabilities. Your criterion would conclude that no action should be performed to satisfy the appetites and excessive use of the senses. So, my friends, your criterion involves more than temperance; it also includes abstinence.

XARGOS.— What a mess we've made! I assume you have a solution to this problem, right?

MARA.— I can think of a way to justify the opposite argument. Isn't an appetite an alteration of the order of the body or mind, that prevents it from performing the rest of its functions normally? If we regard this alteration as a disorder caused by the natural order, then satisfying the desire will restore order to the body and mind. According to everything you've said about order, it should be right to satisfy the appetite. What happens then?

HERMES.— Good question, but I think I have the answer. Both ideas are certainly incompatible, so there must be an error in one of them. To my way of thinking, it would be the former, since you didn't apply the criterion rigorously enough. No one would hesitate to eat if they were hungry. Now the problem is to discern when it's right to satisfy our appetites and when it's not, and we want to use prudence to solve this. As Mara pointed out, that means using the criterion we established. I think this procedure is simple for hunger and thirst. We know that when our bodies ask for food or water, they are fighting an internal battle against the natural order, and we should undoubtedly decide to satisfy them. But let's apply the criterion more rigorously. The objective is to satisfy the appetite called hunger, so we would perform the action of eating, which we'll assume is the one requiring the least effort. We then have to imagine the opposite action, which would return us to our initial state. The actions we could think of might include trying to turn back time, vomiting, or simply waiting long enough to feel hungry again. This is where I think Mara made a mistake because she didn't seek the action requiring the least effort to achieve the opposite objective. Of all the opposite actions, waiting requires zero effort. Of the two actions, we should perform the one requiring the most effort, which is to eat. But this conclusion is the least interesting of all because all we've really said is that someone who's hungry should eat. I think it's more interesting to know whether we should eat when we're not hungry. So, let's imagine that we have no appetite, and are considering whether we should eat. The objective is simply to eat, and so is the action. Now we have to seek the opposite action or actions and return to exactly the same state, but we already saw that this is impossible. In this case, there's no objective as such, and we already know that we shouldn't perform any action if it's not intended to achieve some purpose. We therefore conclude that we should not eat for the sake of eating.

MARA.— We shouldn't eat for the sake of eating. This path does seem to lead to temperance.

XARGOS.— This last result is no more, and no less, than an application of what we already knew: that we should not act without an objective that's different from the act itself. In other words, the objects affected by the objective are the same ones affected by the action: our body and the food. Before, we had a body without hunger, but with an empty stomach, and an intact apple. Afterwards, we have a body without hunger, but with a full stomach, and a swallowed apple. There's no way to undo the action and turn the swallowed apple back into an intact apple. Because the opposite action requires an impossible effort, we should choose this action as the useful one, and therefore not eat if we're not hungry. It seems that the criterion recommends moderating our appetites and subjecting them to reason, and therefore advises us to be temperate.

MARA.— You said that when the body is hungry, it's because it's fighting an internal battle against the natural order. Why did you say that?

HERMES.— It's true that we haven't provided an explanation for that, but if you'll allow me to leave that matter for later, you'll see that your question is intimately related to the need for appetites. First, let's continue with this fascinating subject you introduced: the virtues.

MARA.— Now I think I understand this criterion Xargos was explaining, the one I decided to call prudence because the definitions were so similar. And I also think it's clear that this criterion applied to appetites leads to the virtue called temperance. Let's try to investigate whether something similar happens with fortitude, which involves defeating fear and fleeing from temerity; and justice, which leans toward giving each party what corresponds to or belongs to them. As we said, a person who has fortitude is someone who defeats fear; in other words, someone who defeats the passion of mind that causes them to avoid or refuse things that are considered harmful, risky, or dangerous. Passion, in turn, is any disturbance or disordered effect of the mind. We can deduce that someone who manages to defeat the disordered mind caused by harmful, risky, or dangerous things will have fortitude. According to your discussion, order must be sought. So, as we can see in our definition, someone who has fortitude avoids a disordered state of mind called fear, and seeks order in their mind. According to our definition, they must also avoid temerity, which I defined earlier as an excessively imprudent action when faced with danger, or an action said, done, or thought without grounds, reason, or motive. According to what you said, your principle suggests avoiding at all costs any actions that are said, done, or thought without a reason. Your criterion therefore leads to fortitude on this path. We defined the criterion itself as prudence, so it's impossible for anyone applying it to commit imprudent acts, meaning that this path also leads to fortitude. All we have to do now is see whether the criterion also prompts the person applying it to defeat their fear. For this to happen, the person using the criterion has to believe in it blindly enough to commit acts that are harmful, risky, or dangerous to themselves or others if required by the criterion.

HERMES.— I doubt that the imperative would lead someone to commit acts like that because if they're harmful, they lead to disorder. If we're never led to such acts, it's not likely to place us in a situation where we'd have to defeat our fear. So, I think fortitude is achieved just like prudence and temperance. But keep going as if I hadn't interrupted; I was enjoying your reasoning.

MARA.— You have me partially convinced, but let's imagine a hypothetical case where such a situation does arise. This is the most delicate part because the person would need to have absolute, blind faith in the criterion. Because different actions must be considered when making decisions, to seek the least amount of effort, compare actions and such, it's normal for our spirit to harbour some doubt. We might be unable to decide for fear of forgetting some action or miscalculating the effort involved. For now, to my way of thinking, the criterion provides a high degree of fortitude, but not 100%. Perhaps we'd have to see whether a religion is capable of inspiring such fortitude, because somehow God would have to negate the fear for someone to blindly take that step. Or He would have to negate the guilt for someone who adopted the criterion called prudence and concluded, based on their knowledge, that they should perform the act, no matter how dangerous, and have it go wrong.

XARGOS.— I agree with Hermes. According to the guidelines we followed to create the criterion, it can't hurt anyone because it moves away from unhappiness globally.

HERMES.— Don't be so sure. The search for order moves us away from unhappiness, but remember, Xargos, that not all order leads to happiness. The criterion enables us to identify order, but does not tell us whether it will be the appropriate order.

XARGOS.— That's true, but now we're talking about creating damage, risk or danger through a conclusion obtained from the categorical imperative. Damage means detriment or destruction of goods; risk refers to the proximity of damage; and danger means a situation that increases the imminence of damage. As we agreed, detriment and destruction are types of disorder. Although our criterion does not ensure happiness, it does ensure order: it cannot lead us to situations where we would have to make use of that last definition of fortitude. I would like to reaffirm that our criterion ensures fortitude.

HERMES.— You've convinced me. I understood it clearly a moment ago, when I reasoned using disorder. My later mistake was to reason generally; in other words, to reason about all types of order accessible to human beings, when we were only talking about avoiding damage, which would surely be avoided because it's a type of disorder. My conclusion is also that such situations would not occur.

XARGOS.— We're back in agreement. Please do continue, Mara.

MARA.— Of course. But first, let me participate in that discussion. What happens when a doctor has to inflict damage in order to save a patient from greater harm? From what you were saying, the criterion would prevent that doctor from acting.

HERMES.— The way you described it, performing the action produces order. It produces the order that would disappear naturally if no action were taken: the harm avoided is greater than the harm produced. The criterion would therefore tell the doctor to act.

XARGOS.— I see the nuance Mara wants to highlight. Even though the criterion itself involves fortitude, the logical relationships that support it do not. How can we be sure that if we don't act, a greater harm will be produced? How can we be sure that the damage we cause will prevent the greater harm? The answers to these questions are beyond the scope of the imperative we're discussing. These types of relationships must be acquired using other procedures, and these are the relationships that harbour and feed doubt, and therefore a lack of fortitude.

HERMES.— The universal categorical imperative, if I may call it that, leads to fortitude. This statement is unequivocal; it is the reasoning used to provide the necessary data that does not possess fortitude. The fortitude for that reasoning must be acquired through the act of faith that Mara was alluding to. In this case, however, fortitude and prudence are contradictory. Prudence will tell us not to act because we don't know exactly why we're doing it: we don't know the scope of our action, and fortitude seems to be telling us to act. So, using fortitude in this context, where there is a lack of information for decision-making, is itself a lack of virtue because it contradicts prudence. Only when sufficient information is available for prudence to decide should we make use of fortitude in order to act accordingly. This is not a problem with the criterion we're applying, but with the confused person who insists on using fortitude to make decisions without sufficient knowledge.

MARA.— We still have to decide whether the person using the proposed criterion, or prudence, will be just. To me, this seems like it could be the most delicate subject because it involves third parties and the information we have on them. But let's imagine that we have sufficient information to be sure that something belongs to someone, and if we don't give it to them, we are acting unjustly. In this case, the objective pursued is to be just. To do so, we want to perform an act that involves giving someone what corresponds to or belongs to them. If this objective is not met, we would be acting unjustly. This is what happens when our action is to not give someone something that belongs to them. If we doubt whether we should give them the object, it's not because that object has any value for us. If we give it to that person, we lose any value it may have had, and we'd have to make an effort to return the object we've given. If we don't give it to them, we won't have to make any effort. Of these two situations, the one requiring the greatest effort is the first one, so we should conclude that the correct action is to give the object to the person it belongs to. In other words, the criterion adopted will make the person applying it just.

HERMES.— This time, I think you were carried away by euphoria. We're all hoping our criterion will make the people using it just, but we can't let ourselves get carried away by our excitement and stop using the criterion correctly. In your reasoning, you didn't consider an action and opposite action, but the action of giving and the option of being passive by not giving. We already know that being passive is not good, but that doesn't mean that acting is good. As Mara pointed out, acting was associated with more effort than not acting, which is logical, but we know nothing about whether the effort we make to act will contribute to generating order or disorder. If the action creates order, perhaps it should be performed. If it creates disorder, it should not. To be just, the necessary action is to give each person what corresponds to or belongs to them, meaning that the object given goes from us to its rightful owner. The object affected by the objective is ours in the initial situation, and not ours in the final situation. To undo the action, the object must return from the recipient to us. For that to happen, we would have to seek certain opposite actions such as buying it, stealing it, begging for it, and anything else we can think of. But this entire line of reasoning is incorrect. As you said, Mara, the situation includes a person capable of generating order, like us. So, as we said when we formulated the criterion, in these situations an objective must be sought by common agreement, through dialogue. Both parties would reach a common objective: to be happier, and would decide to act accordingly. One party would then say that being just would make them happier, and the other would say that being treated justly makes them happier, too. They decide to establish the action of giving to each party what belongs to them. By mutual agreement, we would give them the object in question. The object would go from the initial situation of belonging to us, to the final situation of belonging to the person who is its rightful owner. We must now imagine, also by mutual agreement, an opposite action that returns the object to its initial situation of belonging to us. Again, these actions can be to buy, steal, or beg for it. The first involves more effort for us and less for the owner; it would only involve the effort of making the exchange. Theft would not be accepted by mutual agreement, so the dialogue would conclude that giving the object as a gift requires the least amount of effort for both parties. The action and opposite action do not involve the same amount of effort because the action of giving each party what belongs to them requires a preliminary effort to determine whether it truly belongs to them. The other party, in turn, has to make an effort to prove that the object is theirs. The opposite action, giving the object as a gift, only requires that the owner decide to give it to us. We conclude that the action of giving each party what belongs to them involves a greater effort, and that we should do this rather than the opposite action. This is logical; remember that order means to place things where they belong, which means that a more ordered situation is one where an object is with its rightful owner. Now we can indeed say that the criterion leads to justice, and will make the person applying it just.

XARGOS.— I find that amazing. So, a person using our criterion will be prudent, temperate, just, and possess the virtue of fortitude. In other words, a virtuous person!

HERMES.— All this seems amazing to me, too. I never thought we'd get so far. Perhaps the only weak point, to my way of thinking, is the part about fortitude, which was left conditioned by an act of faith. But I don't think it has to be that way. Mara, from what you said, faith is needed to eliminate any possible guilt resulting from making use of fortitude and prudence if the attempt fails. In a humankind where only one person uses this criterion and no one else does, the person who made a mistake would immediately lose heart due to the pressure of condemnation by other people. But where the majority made use of the criterion, guilt would be avoided and replaced by understanding and forgiveness. That was how Xargos and I envisioned it. I think we can also have fortitude simply by believing in the criterion and making a great effort to use it appropriately, by acting as we described earlier when prudence prompts us to act.

MARA.— Maybe you're right. I wasn't here when you discussed understanding and forgiveness. And even if it's not as you describe, that summary is worthy of special mention because it provides a stable action criterion completely in agreement with what is well regarded socially. Not only that, but it's valid for any situation. And if it's not, you should tell it to the engineers. They'd probably find an astonishing similarity between all this and the Second Law of Thermodynamics, which helps them determine what they can and should do, among many other criteria.

HERMES.— Yes, we noticed that similarity when we started our dialogue. But now I'd like to finish with another direct application of the criterion. When you were talking about justice, you concluded that the criterion would ensure that being just would be the option chosen. In other words, giving each party what belonged to them. But it's amazing that the result would've been the same if you'd described justice this way: giving each party what they need. Similarly, prudent people, as you called them, Mara, should tend to share what is theirs with other people, their direct assistance, money, time, food, or knowledge. There is undoubtedly a limit: you can't cross the boundary that endangers your own bodily or mental order, or that of those around you.

13

On moderation in the use of resources – the professions

The professions prevent disorder and increase efficiency.

This statement is objective, global and universal.

MARA.— Of course, as we said, endangering someone's physical or mental health is a kind of disorder. The criterion itself should prevent that.

HERMES.— It will only prevent that if our own well-being is always among the objectives. It's obvious that it is. In fact, it's an objective implicit in all our actions. But for the imperative to realise that it exists, it must be considered explicitly.

MARA.— In other words, without that objective, the fundamental need to not be passive, imposed by the criterion, would lead us to exhaustion. If we were clever, we would include our own order among our objectives. In other words, in order to avoid exhaustion, we would have to be selfish, which doesn't seem very virtuous at first glance. If that were the case, to continue to be virtuous, we would have to throw ourselves into an endless frenzy of actions.

XARGOS.—This action doctrine seems rather dangerous to me. If we followed the path of greatest effort in all life situations, wouldn't we end up breathlessly perishing, overwhelmed by a staggering number of tasks? I'm asking you this because even though we said we should be efficient, the search for happiness is based on acting correctly, avoiding those decisions that require minimal effort. In other words, it consumes resources. We also have to act continuously to deal with the outside world and meet the objective of creating order.

HERMES.— In this sense, we mustn't forget that a good decision must always be made while assessing our strength. A choice that endangers our physical or mental well-being would not be the right one because, according to our own guidelines, a deterioration of the human body is a type of disorder that must be avoided.

XARGOS.— So, I understand that you're establishing a hierarchy, or different levels, among the different types of order that can be achieved, depending on the object affected.

HERMES.— I think so. If you agree, let's make an initial observation about this hierarchy. When in doubt about what to do first, whether to order or keep our body or anything else ordered, I think we should always choose to order everything, our body and everything else. But if acting this way leads to a situation where the effort required overwhelms us, we should first strive to keep our body and mind healthy.

XARGOS.— That seems like a selfish position. Isn't selfishness an immoderate and excessive love of oneself, that causes one to attend disproportionately to one's own interests, with no concern for others?

MARA.— You guys brought a dictionary!

XARGOS.— Hermes brought it. Answer me, isn't that selfishness?

HERMES.— If we analyse it simplistically, it might seem like a selfish position. But I think it's the best of all positions, and it's not selfish at all. To not be selfish, we have to help others. The person best able to help others has a perfectly healthy body and mind. Making sure we do everything we can to maintain our bodily and mental order is the best position in order to offer others our most effective help when they need it. In this sense, established rest periods must be taken with pleasure. Hours of sleep and meals must not be missed, and vacations and weekends must be enjoyed. Those time periods must be used to promote the family, sport, social and other activities that we all need to regain physical and mental strength for our everyday efforts.

MARA.— Here's another approach. If we agree that humankind, taken as a group of individuals, is the group with the greatest capacity to undertake the daring task of overcoming the natural order, then each individual must safeguard their own well-being and everyone else's in order to not undermine the task. To do otherwise would be to reduce humankind's ability to generate order.

XARGOS.— You've convinced me. First of all, let's safeguard the bodily and mental order of our own body. Actually, I think you convinced me because I already thought that way. In any case, I don't think that establishing hierarchies now would be a firm foundation for creating a solid link, since a hierarchy can be easily criticised. I don't agree with this direction we're taking, but I'm still intrigued about the result. What do you think should be the second level of the search?

HERMES.— Well, now that we've established that our bodily order is the most important thing, and since we'll surely find ourselves in situations where we don't have the strength to achieve it, we'll need help from others. In order for this help to be effective and efficient, they must also find themselves as ordered as possible. I think the second level is for us to safeguard the bodily and mental order of everyone we encounter on our path.

XARGOS.— Let's accept that as you explained it. Although if we start judging the bodily and mental order of the people we encounter on our path, we could commit all manner of injustices and vain judgments that would make us their enemies. What a way to seek happiness! So, allow me to ask you in jest, what's the third thing we should seek?

MARA.— Don't be so sarcastic. The dialogue you spoke so much about prevents such injustices. It's true that Hermes is not deducing this hierarchy rigorously based on the imperative you formulated, but that doesn't mean that what he's saying isn't true. We can apply the criterion rigorously later to verify it. Go ahead, what's the third thing we should seek?

HERMES.— I'm not sure, but I think it should be all those actions that prepare us to practice our profession, whatever that may be, with the best possible result.

XARGOS.— Practicing a profession is a task requiring a great amount of effort. So, if we're going to apply the criterion roughly, it seems logical that it should be one of the things we seek. And now that I'm approaching this subject differently, I think all professions seek to increase order in some object. Medicine seeks to maintain order in the human body; psychology and psychiatry, in the mind; engineering, in our surrounding environment; lawyers, politicians, police, and the army, in the social order; theology, in the spiritual order; art, in the aesthetic order; street sweepers, in the order on the streets; and professors, in the intellectual order needed to live in harmony and practice one's corresponding profession.

HERMES.— I think we've had enough lists. Now that you mention it, I agree that all professions seek to increase order in some object. And right now, I can't conceive of any profession that generates disorder.

XARGOS.— So, each person doing their job should feel content with the work performed, and seek the means to improve upon it.

14

On the need for the existence of appetites

The appetites, moderated by reason, minimise disorder in the body. This statement is objective, global and universal.

XARGOS.— Now I remember that we left a couple of issues without a satisfactory conclusion, at least for me. You promised to talk about why the body, which is ordered, does not go against the natural order. That was when we were discussing leg hair removal, remember? You also promised Mara that you would explain why the body is waging a battle against the natural order if it has an appetite. You also said that the natural order requires the existence of appetites.

HERMES.— To answer those questions, we should start by recognising that appetites are impositions we receive directly from the natural order. As beings immersed in the Universe, we are also necessarily subject to its laws. The natural order manifests itself in us by producing illnesses, but also by the need for appetites: hunger, thirst, sleep, sex, and breathing, breathing which would also be an appetite if death by asphyxiation didn't happen so swiftly.

XARGOS.— How can you conclude that appetites are necessary based on the premise that human beings exist immersed in the natural order? By starting with the existence of a Universe as we know it?

HERMES.— Well, the answer is apparently simple. We've stated, and I think we all agree, that the natural order causes all sensory objects that are not in contact with anything else to move toward disorder. So, if this is true, isn't it strange that there are certain structures that are born daily, and become more ordered as the days pass?

XARGOS.— But of course! That was the question I asked you earlier.

MARA.— You're obviously referring to living beings?

HERMES.— That's right. Let's look at humans in particular, since they concern us the most. Two gametes engender a zygote that starts multiplying at the cellular level, increasing its complexity and therefore its order. For many who have not listened carefully to our definition of the natural order, this would clearly be a counterexample that would allow us to state that the natural order is not the same for all sensory beings. They'd claim that this is the case because we found a group of cells ordering themselves against what the natural order would want. Well, the fact that the group of cells orders itself does not violate the natural order. The explanation lies in the fact that an embryo does not grow in an isolated environment, but rather inside its mother. The mother is an ordered, stable structure throughout her maturity, unless she is unfortunate enough to become ill. Here we can ask ourselves what came first, the chicken or the egg. In our case, it was obviously the mother, so let's focus our questions on her. How is it possible that the mother, who is an ordered structure, is not forced into disorder by the natural order? Well, this is due to the fact that she maintains the order she needs by generating much more disorder than the order created. A mother or any other adult organism is therefore a disorder factory, as required by the natural order.

MARA.— I don't quite understand. Please elaborate.

HERMES.— All right, I'll try to explain it more clearly. Let's accept that the natural order tends to move toward disorder, and let's accept the possibility that the natural order sometimes behaves by creating very little order and a lot of disorder. If we were to combine the small amount of order created with the large amount of disorder produced, the mixture would be predominantly disordered, so we wouldn't have violated the natural order. Now let's imagine an organism that has somehow learned to separate that small amount of order created from the disorder. Once it has separated the two, it expels all the disorder and keeps the small amount of order obtained for itself. Obviously, this type of process requires an effort. This is why appetites exist. Appetites are necessary for the organism to obtain the energy required in the effort of keeping the order needed by the body separate from the disorder it does not need. The body is equipped with a digestive system responsible for extracting the elements it needs from food. The digestive system itself carries out a separation in which the foods are disordered. This provides small elements with a lower degree of order than the complete food, which are ordered, and highly disordered waste expelled outside the body. This process of creating a small amount of order and a lot of disorder is performed by the body as a whole, and by each cell individually. The body must be equipped with organs capable of eliminating all the disorder expelled by each cell. Those organs are the kidneys, skin, and lungs. There are a multitude of organs, such as the heart and the entire circulatory system, whose mission is to ensure the arrival of vital nutrients to the cells, and the collection of the highly disordered waste elements. But let's not get into biological or medical details, since we're not experts on this. Let's stick with the overall picture. The result is that the body has the ability to order itself and keep itself ordered because it is capable of creating some order and a lot of disorder. It also has the ability to separate and expel disorder: sweat, urine, and faeces. Both processes require an effort that forces it to collect foods from the outside that provide it with the necessary energy, as well as previously ordered elements that it wouldn't be able to create itself, such as vitamins.

MARA.— I think I'm beginning to understand what you mean.

HERMES.— When a human being is conceived, the cells start multiplying very quickly. Order is being created, and according to what I just said, an enormous amount of disorder must also be produced, which is expelled. But the incipient embryo still doesn't have an organ capable of eliminating this disorder, or any organ that provides it with the elements needed to sustain the effort required for this ordered growth. Its only possibility of survival is to borrow its mother's organs, which will dispose of that tremendous amount of disorder and provide it with all the food it needs. This preliminary growth process lasts throughout the nine months of gestation. Once this period is complete, the embryo has become a baby with all the organs necessary to eat and expel the disorder it will inevitably generate. That is the moment of birth. During its infancy, the baby undergoes a period of rapid growth and ordering associated with the generation of a large amount of disorder, but its organs are healthy and young, and can assume the task of eliminating this disorder. The body grows rapidly, and the number of cells increases drastically, along with the number of activities performed until it reaches adulthood. At this point, every part of the body subject to the natural order must fight to keep itself ordered. The amount of internal disorder generated by this process is roughly what the body's organs are capable of eliminating, and a relatively stable stage called maturity is reached. Once enough time has passed, the natural order will have taken its toll on different parts of the body, including the organs that eliminate disorder. So, the body that continuously tries to repair itself cannot adequately eliminate the disorder it generates. As a result, the body is poisoned by its own disorder. The resulting process is what we call ageing, which will eventually lead to death. This occurs when one of the vital organs becomes so deteriorated or broken down, in other words, so disordered, that it no longer serves the purpose for which it was structured.

Considering that all individuals of any species will end up perishing due to the disorder that invades everything, the evolutionary process is very slow, slower than I initially thought. For the time being, the species is unable to struggle eternally against the natural order in every individual. And because it knew in advance that it would be unable to avoid the death of each individual, it established the survival of the species through the fertilisation and creation of a new being. Because nature is wise, it chose the time when the body is most ordered for that task, which is during maturity, and instilled the sexual appetite. This is neither more nor less than the body's own way of accepting, in advance, its own death, but not that of the species.

MARA.— That was a simplified, but I'd say illustrative, description of the human body and its evolution. Now that I've thought about it a little more, I can see that because Nature is wise, as you said, it found two paths to the survival of the species. Nature does seem to have known that the death of the individual was inevitable. So, because it couldn't do anything to ensure immortality, it established the sexual appetite, and therefore the continuity of the species. In human beings, it also established intelligence as a means for survival. The progress of reason is also slow, so for now the species survives thanks to procreation, while losing each of its individuals. But perhaps there will come a day when reason discovers how to always keep the individual ordered. That will be the day when the species and the individual never perish.

HERMES.— I don't know. In any case, and leaving aside what could be science fiction, I think we just showed that appetites are *instructions*. They are the obligatory acts that the body must perform to defeat the natural order within itself and within the species. We must therefore respect them, but always subject them to reason. Reason knows when the greatest amount of order is created.

15

On the difficulties with applying the universal categorical imperative

Human beings are finite and their knowledge is fuzzy.

This statement is objective, global and universal.

MARA.— So, shall we play at putting reason to the test, now that it's armed with prudence?

HERMES.— What kind of game are you suggesting?

MARA.— I suggest placing reason before a series of specific objectives, and letting it decide what action should be taken. From what we've said, it's obvious that one should not act for the sake of acting. That means that suicide for its own sake should be eliminated from the actions considered by a human being. But let's try to establish an objective for that action. I suggest analysing the objective of eliminating the guilt that torments us, which has prompted us to consider the action of suicide.

XARGOS.— Let me try. The objective is to eliminate guilt. To do so, the guilt-ridden individual has analysed all the possible actions that could achieve that objective and has concluded that in their case, suicide is the one requiring the least amount of effort. The objects involved are their body and some kind of instrument that would be used to achieve their purpose, such as poison. Before performing the action, the objects would be accompanied by the following attributes: a living, guilt-ridden body and intact poison. Afterwards, we have a dead body and diluted poison. The object directly affected by the objective is the body, so the opposite action would have to restore the body's initial attributes. In other words, it would have to restore the feelings of guilt, after first restoring life. From any perspective, and I think we'll all agree on this, restoring life is an impossible action, and even more so for the person who has already lost it. It requires such a huge, immeasurable effort that it overwhelms the capacities of a human being. In this case, the criterion will prompt us to choose the opposite action, leading us to conclude that we should not commit suicide.

HERMES.— That is certainly the solution. But the way you've approached it, suicide should be ruled out regardless of the desired objective, whether it's eliminating guilt or any other type of suffering. The reason is that the opposite action, which is to restore life, is completely impossible for a human being.

MARA.— All right, it looks like you two were able to handle that problem. But let's see if you can manage this one. A person discovers that one of their objectives in life is to be happy, and concludes that having money is essential for this purpose. So, they decide that their objective is to make money. What should they do?

HERMES.— As we said earlier, the objective of being happy forces them not to be passive. So, having decided not to be passive, they focus their actions on a more achievable objective: making money. Isn't that the problem you're considering?

MARA.— Yes, that's it exactly.

XARGOS.— Let me try to solve it.

HERMES.— You seem quite inspired after all the success you achieved with prudence. We're listening.

XARGOS.— Well, this person's objective is to make money. To successfully achieve their objective, they decide to investigate the actions they can take. After reflecting a while, they decide that they could work or steal. Because this person is accustomed to working, they decide that working requires less effort. Moreover, they decide to work on the farm, which is what they've spent their life doing. They decide to analyse whether working on the farm is the right action, so they seek the objects involved: the fields, grain, machinery, water, the person who buys the grain, and money. After performing the action and analysing the initial and final situations, they conclude that the only object involved in the objective is the money, which previously belonged to the customer, and now belongs to them. They seek all the possible opposite actions, those that could return the object involved in the objective to its initial state, and conclude that the action requiring the least effort is to simply give away the money. So, since it requires more effort to plough, sow, reap, pack, and sell the grain than it does to simply take the money out of their pocket and place it in the buyer's hand, they decide to work.

MARA.— I don't agree. I think there must be an error in Xargos' reasoning because this approach would lead a thief to the conclusion that they should steal. If you remember, when we discussed justice, we concluded that giving something away always requires some effort. If we doubted whether or not we should give something away, it's because the object had some value for us. So, unless I'm completely mistaken, what is the value of the money given away, unless it's used to measure all the effort of ploughing, sowing, watering, reaping, packing, and selling? In this case, the action of working would therefore require the same effort as the opposite action. So, the criterion concludes nothing.

XARGOS.— I think you're right. If the money didn't have that value, why would the person want it?

HERMES.— There's no cause for alarm. As rational people, we can see that even though the value of money should be to pay for the effort performed to achieve it, we lose more than just that effort if we return it. Money is associated with a good difficult to quantify: the possibility of investing it in anything. If we return it, we lose the possibility of purchasing other goods, for example, medicines that we would otherwise have to produce ourselves, which is beyond our abilities. So, if we return the money, we lose more than the effort it took us to achieve it. I would conclude that the opposite action is the one requiring the most effort, and is therefore the one that should be performed. This way, we should not work, and a thief should also not steal.

XARGOS.— I thought we'd found a reliable criterion, but now three different people have applied it to the same problem and reached three different solutions.

MARA.— That's the way it is, and it could be even worse because I still haven't protested about one thing: for some people, stealing could be less costly than working. As you can see, it could get even more complicated.

HERMES.— Obviously, we were looking for the least costly of the opposite actions that would return the money to its original owner. I think we've all reasoned incorrectly because we haven't found the action that requires the least effort. Another way to return the money is by buying something that interests us. In this situation, the money would go back to its first owner, but it would not require as much effort as simply giving it back. If we compare the effort required to earn the money by working with the effort required to return the money by buying something, we conclude that working is associated with greater effort. However, someone who wanted to make money by stealing it would conclude that they should steal.

XARGOS.— I'm getting lost.

MARA.— I don't understand either.

HERMES.— Neither do I. What happened? Why is it so difficult for us to find the solution to this problem, when it's apparently so simple? We have a criterion to apply, but we're not finding a solution. Could the criterion be erroneous in some cases, or maybe we haven't learned to apply it correctly?

XARGOS.— Maybe we forgot some angle when we created our decision-making criterion.

MARA.— I wasn't present during your creative process, but I think the criterion sounds good the way you expressed it.

XARGOS.— I still think the solution I proposed in the beginning is correct.

HERMES.— Why?

XARGOS.— Because it's the same situation we had with the builder. If you remember, Hermes, the builder wanted to know whether he should build a shed, so he considered how much effort it would take to build it and to destroy it, which was the opposite action. He concluded that it would require more effort to build it, and therefore decided to build it. His reasoning was based only on the effort required for the action of destroying. But the way we're reasoning now, he would've thought: the opposite action is to destroy the shed. The associated effort is to grab a sledgehammer and demolish the shed, but because I'll no longer have a shed, I'll also lose the value associated with the effort required to build it. So, destroying the shed is associated with more effort than building it. And that, from my perspective, is an over complication that also leads to an absurd conclusion.

HERMES.— You're right. When we assess efforts, we should only consider the efforts associated with the action, and not the value of the objects themselves, which comes from the effort associated with creating the object. From what you just said, both Mara and I were wrong when we associated the value of the opposite action with the value of money. I think we were being too clever for our own good.

XARGOS.— We also have to be careful with how we phrase the problem. Obviously, the solution depends on how the problem is approached, which in turn is nothing other than the objective. Let's suppose that for problem one, the objective is to build a shed. For problem two, the objective is to keep the tools indoors. The opposite action for problem one is to destroy the shed, and the opposite action for problem two is to take the tools outside.

MARA.— Xargos mentioned stealing and working as possible actions for getting money. Couldn't someone think that stealing requires less effort than working?

HERMES.— Yes. In fact, that does happen. People steal because they find it impossible to find a job that provides them with the same amount of money for the same effort.

MARA.— If I'm not mistaken, the criterion says nothing about how to choose between stealing and working, except that we should choose the option requiring less effort. It only helps us choose between working or not working, or stealing or not stealing.

HERMES.— It seems that in the time we spent discussing virtues and the human body, we forgot how to apply the criterion correctly. This is undoubtedly a product of the natural order, which has managed to disorder our minds with forgetfulness. Let's not give up. Let's make an effort to order our intellect once again by reviewing all the important points we covered tonight. One was that if our objective was mixed with the purposes or objectives of another being, we should engage in a dialogue in order to establish a common objective. We also know that if no objective is established, we should not act. So, stealing would surely be eliminated from the possible actions because once a dialogue was established, the victim would never be persuaded that the theft would be in their best interest. If no common objective were reached during the dialogue, the thief should not act as we've described. If he still chooses to act, his action will create disorder, thereby moving humankind a little bit farther away from happiness.

MARA.— So, after several attempts, we conclude that Xargos' first reasoning was correct, meaning that we should work to get money.

HERMES.— That's right.

MARA.— After this little mess we've made, I almost don't feel like playing anymore.

XARGOS.— Don't be like that, Mara. I'm still enjoying this.

MARA.— OK, let's see if you manage to enjoy this new problem. A man is considering cutting down a forest to get cheaper wood.

XARGOS.— Let me do it; this one's a piece of cake. The objective is to get cheaper wood, and the action requiring the least effort is to chop down the forest. The object included in the objective is the wood from the trees, which is alive in the forest in its initial state, and dead in the man's possession in its final state. The opposite action is to return the wood to the trees and create a living forest, which is impossible. Therefore, he should not cut down the forest.

HERMES.— All right. But where do we get the wood to make furniture?

XARGOS.— Don't argue with me; I'm only applying your criterion.

HERMES.— So now it's mine. A while ago it was everybody's.

XARGOS.— Yes, but a while ago it wasn't giving us so much trouble.

MARA.— Well, guys, I'm loving it. We managed to save the forest thanks to our criterion. That's what I was hoping to do: save nature.

HERMES.— This is not a matter of hope; it's a matter of reasoning.

XARGOS.— Hey, let's not ruin it right at the end. I think the natural order is starting to get to us, and is leading us down the path of disordered discussion rather than ordered dialogue. I'd like to propose another problem for you: to convince someone of something, and get them to change their mind, should we engage in dialogue, argue heatedly, or use force?

HERMES.— You certainly have learned a lot about stating problems. That type of problem can't be solved with our criterion!

XARGOS.— What a crappy criterion then!

HERMES.— There you go again. If you don't stop that, tonight will end badly.

MARA.— Come on, guys. I'm using my very sweetest voice to try to calm this temperamental mood that's come over you for absolutely no reason. We've been engaged in dialogue for hours with no problems, especially you two, and I see no reason why things should become heated right at the end. All I can think of is that perhaps tiredness is diminishing your faculties for maintaining the order that the situation requires.

HERMES.— That's true, let's be prudent and seek more order than disorder. But first, Xargos needs to apologise for describing my criterion as crappy when it's not even finished yet!

MARA.— Now I'm going to get upset! Can't you guys set aside all those disorders of the mind, such as pride, and continue our dialogue while seeking the common order, and therefore happiness, instead of looking out for your own ego? You're acting like little kids who still haven't realised that they're immersed in a natural order that tends to disorder them. Be strong, or shall I say virtuous, and don't go along with the natural order.

HERMES.— All right. Xargos, we have a serious problem on our hands, which is the one you just proposed. If you still feel like solving it, we can try it together.

XARGOS.— That sounds like a great idea.

HERMES.— If I remember correctly, it was about convincing someone of the truth, right?

XARGOS.— That's right. Suppose, Hermes, that you're in possession of the truth, and that I, Xargos, am not. Your objective is to order me by sharing the truth with me, and persuade me to change my mind by moving me away from my supposedly false truth.

HERMES.— The action I'd establish would be to successfully convey my teaching to you. I would then realise that you're a person perfectly capable of creating order, in which case you'll certainly have your own objectives, which could interfere with mine. I'd therefore start a preliminary dialogue, in which I'd try to persuade you that I think you're in error. My objective would be to get you to change your mind. What would you tell me during that dialogue?

XARGOS.— I'd tell you that I'm the one in possession of the truth, and that you're in error. I'd then take advantage of the situation to try to convince you of that. You might say that I'd make convincing you that you're wrong my personal objective. However, when I started the dialogue in order to achieve that objective, I would realise that you, like me, are also capable of generating order, and might have your own objectives that could conflict with mine. So, I'd also try to start a preliminary dialogue in order to seek a common objective.

HERMES.— From that preliminary dialogue that we both started, couldn't we reach the conclusion that a common objective for both of us would be to find the truth?

XARGOS.— Yes. That way, Hermes and Xargos would have a single objective: to find the truth, regardless of which of the two might have been right or wrong initially. With a little luck, one of us might be in possession of the truth. But the most likely scenario is that neither of us would be right, and we'd find a much more accurate truth together than what we possessed initially.

HERMES.— You're right, that's probably what would happen. So, our problem is actually to achieve the objective of finding the truth, and the actions we could propose are observation, dialogue, discussion, confrontation, experimentation, study, and all or some of these at the same time.

XARGOS.— At this point, we should seek the action or combination of actions that would require the least amount of effort to meet our objective. I don't know what actions you think we should choose, but I do know which one we shouldn't choose.

HERMES.— I think I know where you're going with this, but go ahead.

XARGOS.— From the moment we adopted the same objective, to find the truth, we would behave like a single being that's increased its capabilities by multiplying them by two. A single being seeking the truth would never choose something that constituted a nuisance or caused them to lose strength as a means to achieving an end. Similarly, we would conclude that heated discussions or confrontations only involve more effort than dialogue to reach the same objective. In that case, fighting and confrontation are actions that should not be chosen when dialogue requires much less effort.

HERMES.— I agree. That means we still have to discover the truth using the other actions: observation, experimentation, dialogue, and study. Assuming that we've used them as efficiently as possible and have managed to find the truth, both of us will change our minds immediately and believe in that truth. The object involved in the objective is our intellect, which is far from certainty in its initial state, and has achieved certainty in its final state. What would be the opposite action that would return our intellects to their initial state?

XARGOS.— It would be sufficient for us to listen to any unfounded opinion different from ours and adopt it without thinking, either by following our intuition, out of sympathy, or for any other frivolous reason. That way, we would abandon the truth and move toward a situation that would be farther removed from it.

HERMES.— Without a doubt. We'd see that finding the truth would involve more effort than abandoning it, and we'd conclude that we should seek the truth together.

XARGOS.— Yes. We now know by common agreement that we should seek the truth to find happiness, and that discussions, confrontations, and fights should be ruled out as ways of achieving that.

MARA.— Bravo! Watching you two construct is much more gratifying than watching you argue. So, now that we've put the philosophy back into our game, here's another problem: The objective is to cure a patient who lives in New York, but the person who wants to achieve this is an explosives expert and member of a strange sect. They decide that to cure the patient, the action requiring the least effort is to place a bomb in Tokyo that will completely destroy the city.

XARGOS.— An interesting problem. Nobody would do that.

HERMES.— Don't be so sure. There are billions of human beings. Surely one of them could get carried away by the natural order, and end up thinking that way.

XARGOS.— Let me solve this one. The objective is to heal a patient who lives in New York. The action that our healer is considering is to destroy the city of Tokyo using a bomb because that's the action that requires the least amount of effort for him. The object involved in the objective is the patient, who is ill in the initial situation and healed in the final situation – at least, in the mind of this healer. The opposite action is one that would make the patient sick again, which could probably be achieved simply by waiting until that happens. The healer concludes that producing the bomb, taking it to Tokyo, placing it there, and managing to totally destroy the city requires much more effort than waiting, so they decide that what they should do is completely demolish the city of Tokyo.

MARA.— But that conclusion is crazy!

HERMES.— Yes, but the criterion reaffirms it.

XARGOS.— There's something fishy about all this. We could commit all sorts of acts of madness if the problems are not well stated. Once again, I think the criterion contains some kind of error.

HERMES.— Maybe so, but it worked quite well in other cases. This one is so strange that I need some time to figure out what's going on.

MARA.— Couldn't there be some situations where it's not applicable? It certainly seems like a powerful tool, but maybe it's not universal and doesn't work with all problems. In fact, the way it's phrased, it only helps us determine whether to perform an action or the opposite action, which is the same thing as not performing the action. The criterion doesn't help us find all the possible actions. And it doesn't help us find all the opposite actions, or establish an objective criterion to determine which action requires the least effort.

HERMES.— I agree with your way of looking at the problem, and I think you're very close to a solution. The criterion is not capable, on its own, of finding each and every one of the possible actions that can be taken to meet an objective. It's easy to see that they would probably be very numerous and difficult to imagine, even in the simplest situations. We'd have to find them some other way. And it doesn't tell us how to determine how much effort is required to undertake a particular action, which we'd also have to judge in some other way. But it does tell us which action to choose: the one requiring the most effort, in an efficient manner. So, to apply the criterion, we need knowledge provided by prior experiences, by dialogue with people who've been in similar situations, and by study. In general, there are certain types of actions for which the decisions are conditioned by knowledge acquired through a trade, at teaching institutions, or at universities. It seems unquestionable that there are professionals who have amassed the necessary knowledge on a subject, to the point where they can find the actions and opposite actions and assess the effort required.

MARA.— It seems obvious that the conflict arose when the healer, who is not a healthcare professional, tried to heal the patient by seeking the possible actions among his intuitions, beliefs, and personal opinions. If this same problem were considered by a physician, which is what usually happens, he would seek the actions provided by the study of medicine. He would study experiences amassed by all of humankind on how to heal the sick. He would see that these do not, and will never, include the option of placing a bomb in Tokyo because there is no causality of any kind between the bomb and the patient.

HERMES.— It does seem obvious that the criterion can't solve problems all by itself. It's definitely the right tool, but it requires outside information on causalities and required effort in order to undertake an action.

MARA.— We already noticed that when we discussed fortitude.

XARGOS.— The tone of our conversation seems to indicate failure, but nothing could be farther from the truth. We've learned a lot tonight, and we've created a very powerful procedure. The same criterion showed us that we shouldn't be passive, but also that we shouldn't act for the sake of acting. It taught us that someone using it appropriately has a good chance of becoming virtuous, and that the professions are necessary to avoid absurd conclusions when using the criterion with certain objectives specific to those professions. And have you forgotten how these problems are resolved? If that man had actually applied the criterion, he never would have planted the bomb, no matter how much he believed in it. He would have been forced to engage in a dialogue with the people of Tokyo.

MARA.— I think you're right.

16

On the scope of the universal categorical imperative

Correct, systematic application of the universal categorical imperative reduces the fuzziness of humankind's ethical knowledge.

This statement is objective, global and universal.

'It does seem obvious that the criterion can't solve problems all by itself,' were practically the last words he said. Now they were all silent.

He certainly felt rather discouraged. Disappointment and euphoria were running through his now-tired head in a disorderly fashion. At some moments, he felt proud to have made as much progress as he had. At others, he could scarcely overcome the difficulties that had taken hold of his heart. His heart that had been full of hope in the beginning, but now harboured doubts.

Two were now crowding his mind. First, it was impossible for one hundred per cent of humankind to think the same way. Second, other studies were necessary in order to properly apply the supposed law they had created. He considered the matter further. Such study was required for two reasons: first, to be conscious of the common sense that led us to the natural order; and second, because we must know what possible actions exist and the effort they require. This involves an initial study to achieve the former, and a lifetime of study to achieve the latter.

That was the pessimistic part, but the optimistic part came as suddenly as the pessimistic thoughts retreated. But of course! It's true that we probably wouldn't reach one hundred per cent of humankind, but surely it would be the great majority: ninety, ninety-nine per cent? The only way to know would be to begin the application.

And how could other people begin applying it, if they themselves had found it difficult to use? They had encountered so many pitfalls. Had they all been overcome? Discouragement found its way back to heart, as if it had been a constant presence.

He felt obligated to act: I must review everything we've said, fix it, and dress it up so it can be conveyed. Should I do it?

He remained lost in his thoughts. Suppose I do it. I would first have to engage in a dialogue with everyone to establish the common objective; discovering whether this is the right path. We would then need to engage in a dialogue in order to convey the information. The opposite action, returning everyone to their initial state, could prove much more costly because if we're right, convincing the majority could prove impossible. If convincing people of a truth is costly, convincing them of a lie must be even more so. I must therefore choose not to convey this information.

Despair was taking hold. He remembered how Xargos and he had discussed trying to change people's minds, and had concluded it should be done through dialogue. A while later, dialogue was not the answer. The reason was obvious: the opposite action they were using then was different from the one he was using now. The one they were using earlier was to simply accept what we are told. Then it had only been the two of them deciding what to do, but many people would now demand to know why they should change their minds again, and accept something known to be a lie. Why should they change their minds when someone is deceiving them? The key is the effort required to recognise the trickery. To simply accept the lie involves zero effort, and also saves them the trouble of determining whether they are being tricked. That means that no effort is involved for them, or for me, to accept any opinion as true. What does require more effort is to get them to *want* to accept it. I can simply make up something, anything, that involves very little effort for me, and let them decide to believe on their own. So, I *should* convey the information. After all, I can succeed in what I was hoping to do.

MARA.— You have disappointment written all over your faces. What's going on?

HERMES.— I'm not convinced by what we've done. I'm running out of steam.

XARGOS.— We may have been too ambitious.

MARA.— I don't think so.

XARGOS.— When we started, we had nothing. Now we have something. However, I can't quite see what's missing for me to feel completely convinced.

MARA.— You look like you've been defeated. The difficulties we've had are only caused by the fact that we haven't properly assimilated this way of thinking. We're like chicks hatching from eggs. We still have a long way to go.

HERMES.— During this last silence, the same thing happened to me. I ran out of steam trying to solve a problem that we'd already solved.

MARA.— That's normal. Our intuition led us down this path. Whoever follows us won't have to make the effort of following their intuition because we already did that; they can focus their efforts on its maturation. And whoever follows them will find that the way has been paved, and they'll be able to begin using it systematically. Whoever follows them will inherit an everyday thing, and it won't cost them any additional effort to use it on a daily basis.

XARGOS.— So, we'll have to wait at least three generations to see if what we said was the right path.

HERMES.— It's like that story about not counting your chickens before they hatch.

XARGOS.— I don't think it's a story. We defined what has to be done, and a creative process like that is very costly, but learning to apply this thinking correctly is even costlier. I agree with Mara. It might need to mature for a long time before it can be refined. And I don't think we're failing; we just don't have all the information we need to apply it correctly. We don't know the infinite set of actions that human beings can perform, and we don't have a general, objective method for measuring the associated effort. That's where the problem lies, not in the criterion itself.

MARA.— I repeat, the only problem is that it is still not assimilated. Creating might be a relatively long process, but assimilating what you've created is a very long process indeed.

HERMES.— I'm suddenly finding it easy to understand that this universal categorical imperative is part of our entire way of thinking, from *Thou shalt not kill* to *Do not do what you do not want to see become a universal law*, and continuing with the need for dialogue and respect for others.

MARA.— To put our minds at rest, let's try to prove that it is already part of our way of thinking. I propose the objective of killing someone who's bothering me. The action I'm considering is to murder that person. In this case, that's much less costly than convincing them not to bother me; otherwise, I wouldn't consider killing them. I imagine them dead, and now I'll have to undo the action to restore the annoyance. Because it's impossible for me to bring them back to life, the effort of the counteraction exceeds the effort of the action, so I decide that I should not kill them. See, the criterion is valid. We can replace a set of recipes with a universal criterion. That's very important.

XARGOS.— Not only is it important, it's the way forward: it's universal ethics and morals. Dialogue and respect are other outcomes, as we've seen throughout our night together.

MARA.— *Do not do what you do not want to see become a universal law* or *Do not do as you would not want done to you* are also maxims included in this ethic. Because the criterion seeks to move us away from unhappiness, it inhibits that which we would not want done to us. And it does so in a global manner because dialogue includes both of these maxims, and dialogue is generated by our criterion.

XARGOS.— We could keep searching...

MARA.— And not only in general cases; it also works in more particular cases. Gender violence, a problem I'm very committed to solving, is repudiated by the imperative. Beating one's mate is unthinkable for someone whose intellect has grasped the scope of the criterion: the preliminary dialogue would prevent it, and so would the knowledge that the blows would only cause disorder in a previously ordered body. According to this criterion, violence is not the way forward because it moves us away from order, and therefore from happiness. So, we can see that violence can't withstand a minimal analysis. If it were considered as a possible action for achieving a purpose, it would be ruled out because an objective requiring violence can only be, according to the very definition of violence, a destructive and destabilising objective that generates disorder.

In any case, those are precisely the objectives that lead directly to unhappiness: we would be helping the natural order to create disorder at a greater speed. Violence is therefore stopped and replaced by dialogue, which we've seen is necessary for eliminating disorder in an effective, efficient, and obviously orderly manner.

And disorders of the mind such as pride, anger, envy, fear, and hate must also be calmed because the criterion says so: anger is the passion of the soul that causes indignation and annoyance. Because passion is a disordered state of mind, it's obvious that anger causes unhappiness. And what can we say about revenge? If revenge is considered as an action for eliminating anger, it's because it's the quickest and least costly path for putting an end to the pain caused by anger. But this path is forbidden by the mandatory dialogue with the person who is the object of our revenge, so the only possibility is not to pursue revenge. That involves having faith in justice for a much longer time than it would take to culminate the revenge. The most efficient way forward, requiring less effort and less wear and tear, is therefore to adopt a serene and determined attitude in support of justice. Once adopting such an attitude becomes our action, we can see that the undo action would be to allow our minds to be taken over by disorderly anger again. This only requires the minimum effort of forgetting the action criterion and our faith in justice. This second path is much less costly than the first, and therefore must be ruled out. And what does the criterion say when revenge itself is the purpose? Revenge is irreversible, and therefore impossible to undo, so the criterion will tell us not to pursue revenge.

That's why the criterion will lead humankind to become more humane, more humble, more committed, more responsible, and more virtuous!

XARGOS.— Applying the criterion to make a decision is a rule or method for doing something, and therefore constitutes order itself: it is close to achieving happiness.

HERMES.— Wow! You guys have boosted my morale. It's funny how after you create something, you always have doubts about its validity. It must be a defence mechanism very helpful for fine-tuning and modelling our criterion. By the way, our criterion was first christened prudence, and has now been renamed as an ethic.

XARGOS.— I don't think I went too far by calling it an ethic. Ethics deals with the morality and obligations of humankind, and morality deals with good in general, and human actions based on their goodness or badness. Ethics describes what good means, and we identified good with happiness, and included happiness within order. This is our ethic. Morality is the practical rule we must use to conduct ourselves in each situation without going outside the ethical framework we've adopted. We introduced the universal categorical imperative, and that is our morality.

HERMES.— Remember how we began by tentatively asking whether there was a universal unifying link? We left religion aside, much to your dismay, and then we left science aside, much to mine. We took what was common to all human beings in the world surrounding them: the natural order. We added common sense as a link and as the heritage of humankind, we related disorder and unhappiness, and we created a method for discovering order. Later, Mara taught us about the scope of our method by applying it to the virtues. This imperative also helped us realise that dialogue is paramount, that we should not act for the sake of acting, we should not be passive, that education and teaching are necessary, and it clearly showed us the need for the professions. And finally, you christened it as a kind of morality.

MARA.— It couldn't have gone any better. If it really is a success, as I think it is, it's because your pillars are grounded in the real world, in the world where we have to act rightly, in the world we all share. I'm happy I decided to come with you.

So Hermes, after a long night, concluded that applying this criterion did require effort. His tired mind was starting to tell him that he'd had enough for today. And he told himself: If we no longer have the same objective, and my will wants to continue, but my mind wants to rest, then it's time to stop. Otherwise, we wouldn't have a common objective, and that would be acting for the sake of acting, which is something we shouldn't do.

Even though he didn't understand it yet, he insisted on applying it. That was probably the problem. But how could he understand something without applying it? That was probably another problem.

17

Goodbye

The universal categorical imperative is a way of proceeding, an order, that can be eliminated by the natural order.

This statement is objective, global and universal.

XARGOS.— If we wrote these dialogues down in a book, what would we call it?

HERMES.— Well, we've been engaged in dialogue, and the object of our dialogue was life and not death. And everything we achieved was made possible by common sense, which is at least partly common to all human beings thanks to the natural order. So, I'd call it *Dialogues on life and common sense.*

MARA.— Even though I was absent for the first part of the dialogue, I think what was created here today is a treatise on tolerance, understanding and union between all human beings. So, I'd call it *Tolerance and understanding: a manual for achieving them.* By the way, it's been a truly extraordinary evening. If the natural order, or whoever, someday decides that our paths should cross again, don't hesitate to ask me to go dancing instead of philosophising.

XARGOS.— Mara, I don't know if you're trying to return our flattery, but I don't think what we did tonight can reach the heights that you're describing. Human beings are, above all, strange, and it's hard to say whether the thoughts that three people had tonight could be thought and understood by each and every other human being. But what worries me the most is whether we ourselves will still think the same way when we wake up in the morning…

Part II

Reflections of an excursionist

Because there were so many, I wanted to write down my reflections.

These are the reflections generated by the conversation I maintained with two people who were previously strangers, one summer night during an excursion. They, Xargos and Mara, went away at the end of the holiday, just like I did. Although we exchanged addresses, who knows whether we'll write to each other or see each other again someday.

It's funny that two strangers can be more effective than two people who know each other when it comes to investigating matters that are delicate or likely to cause conflict. In any case, the conversation provided me with a greater understanding of human beings, and their limitations and greatness, than I have achieved in other settings.

During so many hours of dialogue, there was a succession of feelings and emotions: euphoria and disappointment, camaraderie and individualism. These moods and attitudes followed one another to the rhythm of the apparent successes and unquestionable difficulties that arose while discussing our subject. These ups and downs revolved around a truth that wouldn't quite reveal itself. We got as close as we could, but there was always another step to take, as if we were headed for a dream destination. We were definitely alive while we talked about life: rational, romantic, hopeful, conditioned.

That's why I feel this urgency to preserve a brief summary, as orderly as possible, of what we achieved that night.

At the same time, I'd like to take this opportunity to clarify and expand upon certain aspects that were not fully considered, which are necessary for understanding the scope of the ethic we discovered. This includes the concept of 'fuzziness'.

If I remember correctly, it all started when we asked ourselves whether there was some way to unify the criteria governing humankind in such a way that would cancel out the differences between individuals. My reflections on those conclusions start here.

Reflection One

We agreed that if there were such a thing, it would have to be based on something objective. We discovered that the least subjective definition of order, the one containing the least covenants, states that order is the rule or method observed for doing things.

It is interesting to note that this definition explicitly contains the verb 'do', and thereby recognises humankind's ability to act. It also states that there are rules or methods, in other words, special ways of doing things, and therefore an ability to act in accordance with principles. Finally, the verb 'observe' implicitly assumes the existence of will in human beings, who are able to select a rule or method.

It turns out that these three aspects are precisely the ingredients needed to understand ethics as the branch of philosophy that studies the criteria by which behaviours and choices are evaluated.

Consequently, this definition of order relates the physical world to the ethical world, and is therefore the most suitable for our purposes.

The first advantage cited, objectivity, can be explained by the fact that the definition contains no covenants, except perhaps the very use of the word 'order' for the concept in question. One could object that specifying a rule requires first covenanting on how to proceed, and therefore establishing a covenant. However, it is easy to see that this objection is flimsy because the definition of order proposed is valid for any rule or covenant and, in this sense, is universal. Because the definition used is not conditioned by any agreement that specifies the rule, any action can constitute a rule. The definition is therefore unconditioned.

So, if any action can become a rule, we still don't know anything about the ethical suitability of the rule: a bad rule is just as possible as a good one. Obviously, an ethic for differentiating between them has yet to be built.

Reflection Two

We discovered that the tendency toward disorder is something objective in the natural order, once adequately generalised and abstracted by means of common sense.

Now, this tendency is based on two prior premises. The first acknowledges that the Universe is continuously transforming itself, and the second states that this transformation is beyond the control of our will. If our will establishes order through rules and methods, which necessarily require objects, utensils, situations, temporal patterns, personal attitudes, and a long list of other items, it is easy to see that the mere natural transformation of some of these will cause the rule or method to disappear. What is natural is therefore for the continuous evolution of the Universe to turn our order into disorder. Where a special way of doing things was once accessible, we later lose access.

Let's now examine the meaning of these premises in greater depth.

When we state that the transformation of the Universe is beyond the control of our will, we acknowledge that human beings possess a certain arbitrariness that makes them free. Otherwise, freedom would not exist, and it would be absurd to wonder about the ethical suitability of our actions. If we also add that the Universe is continuously being transformed, then its evolution will surely end up altering our order, our rules and ways of doing things, against our will.

On the other hand, we cannot deduce from the above that the Universe, in its continuous transformation, cannot take an entity sterile for us and turn it into a useful element, so that we can establish a rule or method for doing things with it. However, it is worth noting that the probability of this happening is very low because the number of possible changes leading to something useless is infinitely higher than the number of changes leading to rules and ways of doing things.

Essentially, this is the case because the rules and methods are supported by elements that make it possible to specify and implement them. The elements used must therefore be different from the rest. In other words, if we want our environment to be valid for our purposes, it must be composed of parts of a different nature. Our environment must therefore be heterogeneous.

However, there is empirical evidence showing that in natural evolution, isolated entities tend to become homogeneous. Because there are no differences between homogeneous things, it is also not possible to establish a special way of doing something. Consequently, the number of useless changes will exceed the number of changes that are beneficial for establishing order.

Finally, we can conclude from the above that the natural tendency is toward disorder.

This statement is categorical because it is not conditioned by anything except natural experience and the concept of order.

Reflection Three

We identified happiness as order, in such a way that happiness is not found in disorder.

Indeed, if happiness is the state of mind that delights in the possession of a good (tangible or intangible), then a happy mind will judge that good to be in the place where it belongs. If the good is where it belongs, that is because it allows the will possessing it to establish rules or ways of acting related to it. We can therefore conclude that 'happiness implies order'.

From the above, we can deduce (using the rule of contraposition from logic) that 'disorder implies non-happiness'. Non-happiness is any state of indifference or unhappiness. Indifference describes that state where we can say 'I'm not happy, but neither am I unhappy'.

The most complete connection between order, disorder, happiness, and non-happiness compatible with the statement 'Happiness implies order' (and the opposite) is represented in Drawing 1. This drawing shows that unhappiness and indifference can be reached through both order and disorder, but happiness only through order.

In this diagram, we admit that the search for order would take us farther away from unhappiness if it weren't for the fact that not all order leads to happiness. (It can also lead to indifference or unhappiness.)

DRAWING 1

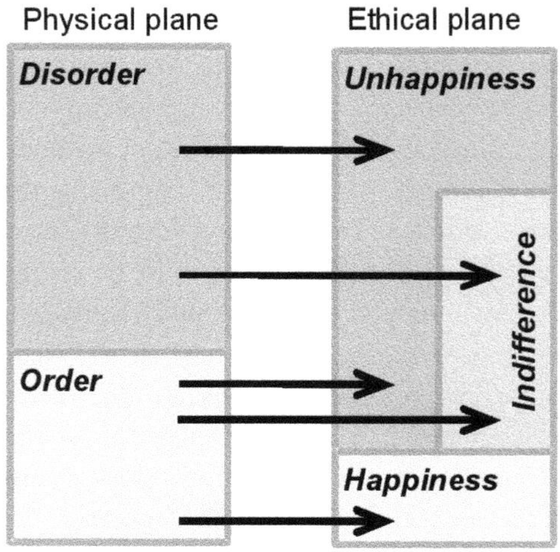

The statement we established, 'Not all order leads to happiness', is based on our acceptance that resources are goods that enable us to establish rules and ways of doing things, and have the ability and power to implement a rule or produce a method.

Let's imagine two actions that lead to the same objective, but consume different amounts of resources. Because any resources consumed in excess will no longer be available, we'll lose part of our potential to generate order in the future, and future rules and methods will disappear. This destruction of order is disorder, so having lost the possibility of using those resources to establish a way of doing something will make us unhappy or indifferent. In other words, it will no longer be possible to use them to produce happiness. As proven earlier (i.e., disorder implies non-happiness), this already constitutes unhappiness or indifference. From the above, we can also deduce that a third action, one that would use the wasted resources correctly, would generate more happiness than either of the two actions proposed above.

With this procedure, we found an action, capable of becoming order, that leads to a lesser degree of happiness the more excess resources are consumed. It's possible to extrapolate the results to deduce that starting from a certain level of inappropriately consumed resources, non-happiness would prevail. This case demonstrates that order does not imply happiness, since it can also lead to either of the other states.

From the above, we can also deduce that seeking happiness requires avoiding those situations that deplete our resources. Because one action is said to be less efficient than another when it consumes more resources to achieve the same objective, we can state that the search for happiness imposes efficiency as the way to ensure a greater measure of happiness. The reasoning followed therefore concludes that to achieve the same objectives, the action consuming fewer resources is the best.

This reflection forces us to regard efficiency as a characteristic to be considered in any ethical evaluation.

On the other hand, if our actions consume resources simply to achieve indifference, we are in a worse situation than when the resources are used to achieve happiness. In this sense, we would be unhappy, and it would therefore be possible to confuse indifference with unhappiness. We can therefore deduce that in a scenario where the resources are limited, or finite, the need for efficiency turns indifference into unhappiness.

The reason for also suppressing the statement 'Indifference can come from disorder' is, again, to accept that resources are goods that make it possible to establish rules and ways of doing things. In this sense, they constitute order that, if consumed to achieve indifference, cannot be used to generate happiness: having the natural order or someone else take away our ability to use those resources to establish a future way of doing something will make us unhappy. This brings us back to the statement 'Disorder implies unhappiness'. Indeed, disorder means taking things away from the place where they belong. In this sense, goods that were producing happiness will tend to move away from the place where they were, disappearing from their 'proper' place. At this point, unhappiness will be the result, rather than indifference.

Consequently, these reflections remove indifference from the ethical plane, as shown in Drawing 2.

DRAWING 2

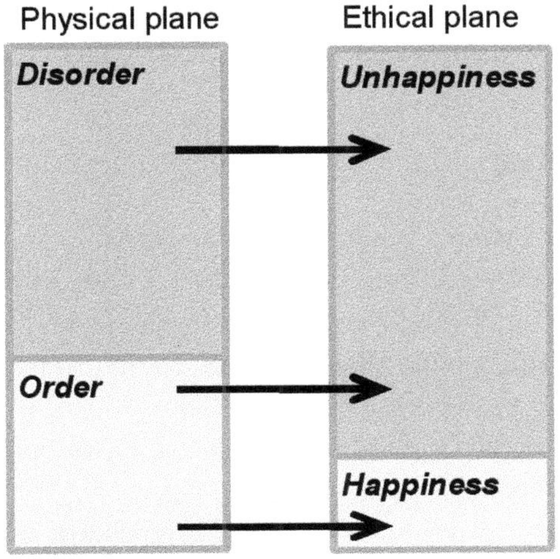

The unconditionality established in the concept of order is inherited by these implications: 'Happiness implies order. Efficiency is necessary to minimise unhappiness or maximise happiness. Disorder implies unhappiness.' Thus, these are unconditionally true, and therefore categorical.

Reflection Four

We discovered that a human being's actions will be characterised by the search for happiness in an environment that evolves by moving toward disorder, as established by the natural order and observed by us. In other words, the interaction between the two parties, human beings and their environment, will define the ethical character of the actions voluntarily undertaken by the former.

The ethic we seek will arise when we recognise the antagonism between two very different evolutions. Human beings evolve by seeking happiness, and therefore order (Reflection Three), and the Universe evolves by tending to undo the order previously established by humans (Reflection Two).

By linking the tendency toward disorder established by the natural order to humankind's search for happiness, the latter is recognised as an integral part of a wider environment, with which it can relate and enter into conflict. The Universe constitutes and envelops humankind. Thus, a human being's happiness is conditioned by the development of the Universe, and the Universe is influenced by the actions of humans. It is therefore understandable that the happiness of human beings is conditioned by the nature of the actions they undertake, and by developments in the rest of the environment.

We can therefore conclude that human ethics arise when human beings acknowledge their relationship to the Universe. This statement is also categorical due to the categorical nature of the statements leading up to it.

Reflection Five

In general, because multiple beings exist in the Universe, unhappiness could be caused if their actions result mostly in disorder for some of them. In particular, it is obvious that an individual's environment includes other human beings, who therefore have something to say about the behaviour of that individual (Reflection Four).

This observation forces us to introduce dialogue as an important part of the decision-making process.

Let's imagine that two subjects undertake independent actions to meet their own objectives. In order to have them interact, let's also imagine that those actions affect the same object. Under these conditions, if one of them acts by transforming the object's attributes, they will ruin what was previously achieved by the other. The first will act again to meet their objective, regaining those peculiarities needed for the object. In this situation, the first subject will have to act for the second time to achieve their goal. This cycle can be perpetuated as long as the available resources permit, but this is obviously not an efficient approach because new resources are consumed each time. Because it is not efficient, it is not ethically correct (Reflection Three).

If one of the subjects realised what was happening and reconsidered how to reach the desired objective, they could avoid this situation as long as the other allowed it. Breaking this dynamic would therefore require mutual recognition of both objectives by means of dialogue. This means that the lack of dialogue, where it is needed, leads to inefficiency. If we remember that inefficiency leads to greater levels of unhappiness, we can conclude that the lack of dialogue, where it is needed, does the same. Finally, dialogue itself determines where it is needed, meaning that we can eliminate the above qualification 'where it is needed'.

The statement 'The lack of dialogue increases unhappiness or decreases happiness' is therefore unconditionally true.

Reflection Six

From an ethical point of view, a group of individuals with a common objective that does not enter into conflict with any other group is no different from a single individual. Actually, we already know from Reflection Four that ethics originates from a conflict with the Universe. So, wherever conflict has been eliminated, there will be no ethical criterion to apply.

In this context, dialogue is defined as the instrument that allows several human beings, whose actions interact, to establish their objectives by mutual agreement. It will therefore eliminate the conflicts existing between the individuals in a group.

However, although dialogue enables a group to establish a common objective for all of its individuals, it does not prevent that objective from entering into conflict with the surrounding environment.

We can therefore deduce that although dialogue is essential, there must be another element that helps us determine whether our actions are correct.

Reflection Seven

Now we'll determine what part of ethics common to groups and individuals was mentioned in the previous reflection.

Because common sense establishes that the environment (of either a group or a single individual) tends to move toward disorder, there is a new aspect to consider in the action criterion. In fact, the order needed to find happiness must be established by actions that impose order where the natural tendency is toward disorder (Reflection Three).

This conflict between human beings and their environment is resolved by the effort that the former must make to impose their will on the course of the latter.

On the other hand, an action resulting in the destruction of order is simpler to perform because our efforts will be augmented by the environment's natural tendency to achieve such disorder. Such an action will be less costly; in theory, it could be achieved without effort, by simply allowing nature to take its course and undo the previously established order.

The fact that human beings seek order and the Universe tends to move toward disorder is the asymmetry ensuring that order requires the greater effort and the consumption of more resources.

At this point, I remember that during our dialogue we only discussed effort, and not resources. However, the connection between the two is established by noting that making an effort consumes resources, so that a larger effort requires greater resource consumption.

Because an action that undoes what was previously ordered is an action that disorders, it must consume fewer resources than an action that orders. Efficiency is responsible for this result. To be efficient, we must make use of the natural order and decrease the resources consumed to achieve disorder. This result will help us determine what is 'correct'.

Again, the ethics of humankind and its individuals arises from acknowledging their relationship to the outside world (Reflection Four). From this relationship, we deduced that dialogue and efficiency are necessary. Now we can also deduce that any action consuming fewer resources, and requiring less effort than the action necessary to undo what was previously done, leads to disorder, and therefore to unhappiness. Similarly, any action requiring greater effort than necessary to undo what was previously done will lead to order, but will not necessarily lead to happiness.

This reasoning, as a system for distinguishing between order and disorder, is categorical. Let's also determine whether it is categorical as a criterion for distinguishing between happiness and unhappiness.

The above procedure, in itself, is capable of identifying a situation of order, but says nothing about the suitability of such order for leading to happiness. Again, the problem lies in the conclusion reached in Reflection Three: not all order leads to happiness. However, the order sought in this case is very special. It is necessary for achieving the objective of the party desiring it without harming third parties, because dialogue prevents that, and without depleting resources, because efficiency prevents that. It is an order reached by consensus, through dialogue, obtained efficiently while also satisfying the volitive desire of the person from whom it originated. We must conclude that such order places its promoter in a happy position because, according to the definition given in Reflection Three, happiness is the state of mind that delights in the possession of a good. Here the good is the order sought to achieve the objective. We can conclude (as long as this person accepts Reflections Three and Five) that the order achieved is such that it satisfies their desires. In this sense, they would possess an intangible good in which they would delight: they would be happy.

Thus, the comparison between efforts described earlier, distinguishes between order and disorder. If we add the other ethical ingredients deduced earlier, and impose compliance at all times, we can also make it distinguish between happiness and unhappiness.

The following propositions are therefore categorical: 'Any action requiring less effort than necessary to undo what was previously done leads to disorder, and therefore to unhappiness', and 'Any efficient action reached by consensus, and requiring more effort than necessary to undo what was previously done, leads to order, and also to happiness'.

Reflection Eight

The statements given in the previous reflections help establish a decision-making criterion that enlightens us on whether our will to act is correct. The following diagram summarises the moral criterion.

The process constituting this imperative begins when a person has an objective in mind and doesn't know whether to proceed. They follow the path marked by the arrows, and reach the end by following two possible routes. One says that the action needed to achieve the objective must not be undertaken, and the other says that something good will be achieved by taking the action.

This action criterion is responsible for determining the ethical result of a particular order.

In this way, the Imperative gives happiness an objective reality, and is a rigorous and stable formula in itself. This objectivity makes it unconditioned in its formulation, and therefore categorical. It is not a maxim, or precept valid for a particular subject, although likely to be valid in most cases. It is a law, or principle endowed with objective validity, and therefore suitable for guiding any rational being through the decisions prompting them to act. Once its unconditional validity is established, it becomes an order, or imperative. Only a practical-formal principle of this kind provides our will with universal validity.

That night, we named this criterion the Universal Categorical Imperative It is an imperative from the very moment it becomes an order that must be obeyed, and is categorical because it is not conditioned by any will, which also makes it universal.

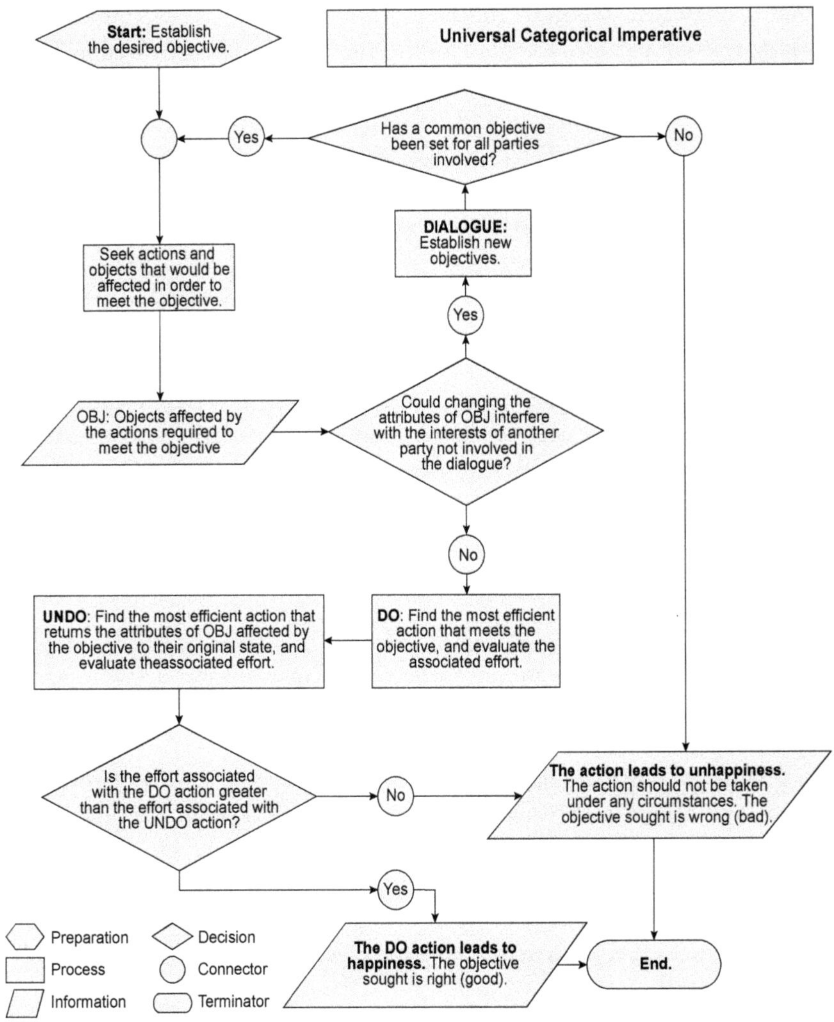

Reflection Nine

Ethics, the theory that describes what is good, is based on the previous steps because it identifies good with happiness, and happiness with a special kind of order on the physical plane.

Morality is the practical rule we must use to guide us through each situation without stepping outside the ethical framework adopted. In this sense, morality comprises the rule that allows us to always seek the appropriate order. In practice, this means using the Universal Categorical Imperative to try to keep disorder to a minimum on the ethical plane.

We should reflect on the difference between the order that leads to unhappiness and the order that leads to happiness. The former results in greater disorder when the whole environment is considered, and the latter minimises the disorder generated. This is how order that considers the outside world can be regarded on the ethical plane, where incorrect decisions generate greater disorder than correct ones.

When humankind's entire environment is considered, the Criterion differentiates between creating disorder and a lot of disorder. In other words, based on the idea that the natural order tends to move toward disorder, it establishes an asymmetry that produces a result.

This asymmetry that differentiates between 'yes' and 'no' shows the non-equivalence between order and happiness. Indeed, as we have shown, there are actions that should not be performed because the Imperative advises against them; for example, any that are less efficient than another. Actions can always become rules and ways of acting; in other words, order. Because some are catalogued as bad once they are subjected to the criterion, we can conclude that they also constitute order that does not lead to happiness.

Thus, it is not surprising that the Imperative itself generates the statement 'Order does not necessarily imply happiness' (Reflection Three). If we also add the expressions 'Happiness implies order; disorder implies unhappiness', we are back to the diagram shown in Drawing 2. However, Drawing 2 does not include the morality established by the Imperative, which affirms or denies whether a specific order leads to happiness. The information added by the Imperative to this drawing therefore indicates which of the two arrows starting from order on the physical plane is associated with our action. This is shown schematically in Drawing 3, where the diamond represents the decision-making process established by the Universal Categorical Imperative.

Reflection Ten

We also deduced that the criterion itself encourages its own use.

Indeed, the very use of the Universal Categorical Imperative requires effort to put into practice, apply and reach a reasoned decision. In this case, the undo action would be to surrender to the arbitrariness of choosing the first convenient action that came to mind without applying any criteria, thus replacing the previously reasoned decision. The undo action obviously requires less effort, and should therefore be ruled out according to the criterion. So, the Imperative is consistent with itself, and the criterion ensures that it must be used.

DRAWING 3

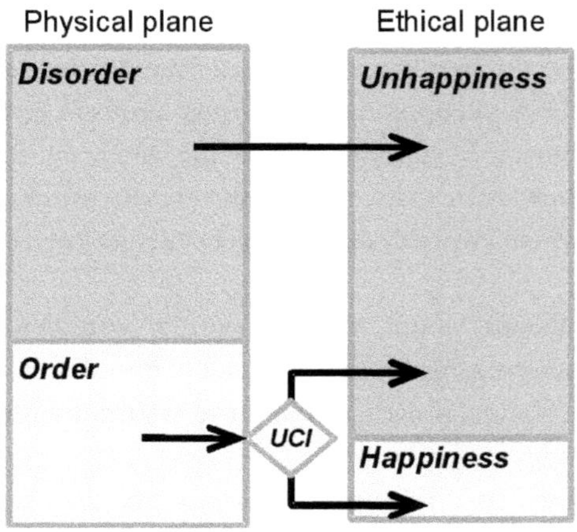

UCI: Universal Categorical Imperative

The systematic use of the Imperative constitutes a rule and a way of deliberating, and is therefore order (shown in light grey in Drawing 3).

This result can also be read another way: because the Imperative recommends its own use, using it systematically leads human beings to situations of greater happiness. It has proven to be order that leads to happiness.

From it, we can also deduce two universal (always valid) statements: 'Don't act if you don't know why you're doing it' (true because it demands efficiency), and 'If you want to be happy, don't be passive, but act' (true because it acknowledges the conflict between happiness and the natural order). These statements summarise the opposite extremes between which the Criterion's flexibility operates. They thereby rule out those criteria that seek happiness based on the minimum effort and those based on the maximum effort, in order to find a path of maximum efficiency in the search for happiness.

Reflection Eleven

We also recognised the need for the professions, and for education in general. Even if all individuals were educated during the early years of their lives in the use of the Universal Categorical Imperative, education would also be needed for them to achieve the following (please use the different steps that appear in the diagram showing the Imperative):

1. To be capable of realising that they wish to meet an objective. This requires at least interest, creativity, and the desire to improve oneself.

2. To realise what actions are accessible for achieving that objective, and what objects are involved. The key words here are analytical ability and know-how.
3. To establish whether any of those objects interfere with those of another party capable of creating order. Critical observation.
4. If so, to establish common objectives. Dialogue.
5. To evaluate the efforts associated with different actions. Evaluation and the ability to formulate judgments.
6. To seek the most efficient action. Objective comparison and an iterative process of analysis and synthesis.
7. To implement the appropriate decision in any case: 'Yes' and 'No'. Willpower.
8. To know how to undertake the action if necessary. Knowledge and ability.

Evidently, in addition to knowledge of the Universal Categorical Imperative, a large amount of information and experience is needed to ensure the success of the process at all times. Given the finite nature of human beings, the accumulated experience of our predecessors must be instilled in our young people as soon as possible. We can therefore conclude that education is vital as a basic pillar of a modern society.

As we are well aware today, education is a procedure for guiding learning. It can be affective, psychomotor and cognitive. The least that should be asked of a person in a position to make decisions involving the ethical or moral plane, or value judgments, is that they must have reached an appropriate level of cognitive learning. Their training should also include the affective level, or human values, and to some extent the psychomotor level, which leads to certain motor skills.

This, in itself, is a restriction. Successfully determining whether a specific order leads to happiness (following the diagram in Reflection Eight), and possessing sufficient knowledge to appropriately follow steps 1 to 8 above, are restrictions to the extent that if they are not adequately understood, they will make it difficult to find a categorical answer.

With the current description of cognitive learning, it is easy to see that the effort needed to completely achieve it is, in itself, a strong limitation making it difficult to properly conclude the application of the imperative discussed here.

Indeed, this is obviously a restriction because to properly complete steps 1 to 8 requires at least an education supporting them with <u>knowledge</u>. A human being's knowledge provides the necessary information required for all other intellectual activities: specific data, vocabulary, terms, properties or facts specific to the surrounding environment; sequences and trends, criteria, methodologies and evaluation techniques; universal and abstract concepts such as principles and theories, lists of laws, formulations, etc.

This data would serve no purpose without a later process of <u>comprehension</u> which, along with the knowledge, produces the lowest level of understanding. One is capable of comprehending the acquired knowledge if one is able to translate the content of the language used into one's own words. One must be capable of switching from one type of language to another, interpreting or reworking the content, and approaching it in different ways. Finally, one must be able to infer new conclusions from the knowledge, which were not previously included in the data.

Without a practical application, the two previous stages (knowledge and comprehension) would be of little use. When the knowledge that was previously comprehended is put into practice, the problem of decision-making arises. In order to approach the problem and its resolution in the most efficient way possible, acquiring a habit is desirable.

The usefulness of the three cognitive structures presented (knowledge, comprehension and application) would be minimal unless the scope, quality and necessity of the ways they are put into practice are continuously assessed. Ensuring that this step is performed correctly requires analysis. The message and its content are broken down into their constituent elements, and the hierarchy and relationships between them are established. This way, the conclusions from the hypotheses and the results of the data can be differentiated based on the elements. During the process of searching for the elements, we can extract links and relationships between them, enabling us to distinguish causes from effects. During this process, we can also extract the principles that allow us to differentiate between what is essential and what is secondary, what is important and what is superfluous.

The next step is a synthesis, a process in which elements are reordered and grouped in order to reconstitute the whole. This is when the creative act can occur, when re-joining the parts can lead to innovation or a new concept, approach or aspect.

The culmination of the entire process is reached in the final stage: evaluation. In order to evaluate, all of the previous stages must be successfully completed. Judgments can then be issued based on both external criteria (the whole is judged based on a comparison with other similar wholes) and internal criteria (the arrangement of the whole is judged based on the harmony between its parts).

So, to put it briefly, the restriction arises from the need to create a world that must educate people capable of properly knowing, comprehending, applying, analysing, synthesising, and evaluating. At the same time, this must all coexist in an individual who has interests and appreciates creativity, self-improvement, observation, dialogue, willpower, and skills.

Because human beings are immersed in the natural order and subject to their own limitations and finiteness, they are imperfect, and therefore unable to completely eliminate the restrictions listed in this reflection. However, this has never stopped the progress of humankind. Any rigour lost has been replaced by an ability to ponder. In this sense, even though nothing was said about this at the time, what we have achieved is obviously a *Fuzzy Ethic*.

Reflection Twelve

The daily operating logic of human beings is fuzzy in nature, or capable of making decisions in uncertain environments. When a question is asked, each answer has a certain weight. Thus, if someone says that the water is cold, we'll make a decision independent of the exact temperature of the water. We'll consider our experience with the person informing us, the time of year, where we are, and how enthusiastic we feel about swimming.

It is precisely this ability to make decisions based on information that is fuzzy, imprecise, and to some extent subjective, that gives these decisions enormous added value when they prove to be right.

The same is true in this case. The amount of knowledge and data needed to accurately apply the criterion is huge. However, the Imperative itself focuses our efforts on those critical points where the greatest attention is required.

If the Criterion tells us not to act, the only uncertainties will be caused by doubts arising from a lack of information for evaluating and comparing efforts. However, if the Criterion prompts us to act, a lack of knowledge for properly undertaking the action is also added. This creates an additional degree of uncertainty that makes the result of this procedure even more unpredictable.

However, the moral tool proposed here provides great value. If implemented within the fuzzy logic natural to human beings, it adds a fuzzy ethic that always points in a direction close to the goal we pursue. When individuals start using it more and more, and it is progressively applied by more people, we'll have access to a greater amount of information on how to use it properly, and the results will become more precise. That is when the ethical growth of humankind will achieve exponential development. This will happen because the Universal Categorical Imperative has established an ethical method.

These final clarifications allow us to state that:

Given the fuzziness implicit to human beings, it will be difficult for the Imperative to unify all criteria governing their decisions in such a way that would cancel out discrepancies between individuals. However, in the context of the fuzzy logic so characteristic of humankind, we emphatically dare say that our Imperative will keep such differences to a minimum.

End of my impressions on what was said that night.

Planet Earth, 23 September, 2000.

Hermes

Part III
Additional content

Using words to explain the tangled nature of humankind's relationship to the outside world requires overcoming the vexation we feel when we discover that it's impossible to write a treatise that would cover the infinite nuances of reality.

Once we accept this impossibility, we approach our task by using the minimum number of different words to characterise the fundamental pillars of that relationship with the most general discourse possible.

However, to ensure that our discourse is also coherent, we must confront some concepts with others until any falsehoods that may be trapped inside are minimised. And to clarify the truth contained in our statements, we must explore the definitions and relationships that bind them.

There is no doubt that the text presented here does not exhaust or fully resolve these questions. The short dialogues contained in this chapter are a good example of this. Each one opens new lines of debate on the meaning of change, society, universality, the Universe, and love. Only a few are included here, but sufficient to show what a labyrinth a detailed description of each concept would be. In any case, the interpretations contained in these excerpts continue to explore, expand upon, and clarify the ideas discussed.

Those readers not seeking greater depth might find a quick read of this chapter entertaining. It shows that there's always so much more to say.

Change

XARGOS.— To identify a good with order, even partially, can seem odd. Order is too rigid a concept for some people.

HERMES.— They might be right. We've already seen that not all order leads to happiness. It would be a matter of applying the criterion to that situation and seeing whether or not that rigid order is correct.

XARGOS.— There are also people who find happiness in the unexpected setbacks on a journey, which are undoubtedly not order for them.

HERMES.— Of course not! As far as whether unexpected setbacks produce happiness when they clearly mean disorder for the journey, we can say that they don't in themselves. They're imposed by nature, which obviously tends to move toward disorder, as we've observed. The happiness provided by the setback probably comes from the way the contingency fits into the overall journey, in such a way that order is obtained where it had just been lost. It is that order arising from disorder that produces the happiness associated with a setback. For those lacking the resources to turn the disorder produced by the misfortune back into order, happiness will not appear, but unhappiness will. There are many examples of this.

XARGOS.— In society, the existence of a legislative order ensures the happiness of many people who feel more protected.

HERMES.— In small children, it's easy to see how unexpected changes in activities can cause confusion and uneasiness. Such changes are a form of disorder, and the inability to turn them back into order is a problem for children.

XARGOS.— The same is true for older people. They find security and peace in order, peace they would lose if there were disorder in their lives.

HERMES.— I don't mean that we should behave in a completely ordered way, performing all our tasks like robots. That would be absurd! Life will continuously surprise us by modifying our paths, and changes should be accepted as such. Some will see reasons for happiness in them, and others will not. Those who do are probably aware that changes are to be expected, although they are unknown and unpredictable. Those who don't will continue torturing themselves with the question 'Why me?'

XARGOS.— In any case, changes place us in different situations where we have to make decisions. No matter how hard we try, life will never stop surprising us. Unexpected phenomena and accidents will take place constantly.

HERMES.— That's when humankind should continue to behave by following a moral criterion that would minimise the effect of those unexpected circumstances.

Society

XARGOS.— Any profession, no matter what it is, makes humankind proud because they all help fight against the natural order.

MARA.— Unless the person practicing that profession is not properly trained. A fraudster or incompetent professional would generate disorder. The former would do so intentionally, and the latter inadvertently.

HERMES.— Justice exists to determine whether that is the case. But that possibility would be remote if everyone were aware of our imperative, and therefore knew that one should not act for the sake of acting.

MARA.— Someone who doesn't know the possible result of their actions cannot use the imperative correctly, and therefore cannot choose a solution.

HERMES.— Even so, if their mistakes led to such an erroneous act, justice would have to assess what to do with that person. But it's obvious that such situations should be minimal.

XARGOS.— It's very easy to boycott the criterion. All you have to do is prevent dialogue!

HERMES.— Yes. We already saw how difficult it would be to fight against someone who did not share these ideas because the imperative requires engaging in dialogue. That's why we concluded that social structures are necessary to maintain order.

XARGOS.— Remember when we said that there was no profession where the goal was not to maintain order?

HERMES.— Yes.

XARGOS.— Well, there are people who consider their purpose to be preventing dialogue. This is easy to see at meetings, board meetings, committee meetings, and parliamentary chambers where certain people are assigned the 'task' of irritating, insulting, making facetious comments, ridiculing, shouting, making time pass, appealing to their own 'right' to defend their position without listening to others, getting cranky, misleading, beating around the bush, introducing erroneous information, discontinuing, proclaiming themselves to be the only ones with the ability and authority, trying not to listen or explain…

HERMES.— It's quite fashionable to act offended for not having been asked first. What's ridiculous is that they do this in precisely those forums where the objective is to debate the issues.

XARGOS.— That's because those people find such behaviour profitable. They prevent the participants in the dialogue, which fails thanks to them, from generating a common objective that would make them stronger. From that weakness, they gain some benefit.

MARA.— That's true. Breaking up the dialogue is not their immediate goal, but it is a useful tool. This method for achieving personal gain basically involves preventing the other party from reaching their goal at a particular time. The return such people gain by using this technique might provide them with a certain satisfaction, but causes others quite a bit of unhappiness.

HERMES.— We already knew it was a bad action policy. It's not ethical. We've proven this by showing that it goes against the Universal Categorical Imperative.

Universality

XARGOS.— How can we know what is right and what is wrong? If most people think that stealing, raping and killing is wrong, couldn't that be because there's something common to all of them that helps them distinguish right from wrong?

HERMES.— What about our criterion? Isn't the criterion itself a definition of what is right and wrong? Couldn't it be considered a right and wrong detector?

MARA.— If I've understood correctly, the adjective 'universal' refers to the general way this procedure for seeking happiness was created. By focusing on an experience that's identical for all living beings, 'the natural tendency toward disorder', it becomes universal. All other decision-making mechanisms created by humankind should fit coherently within this one.

HERMES.— Indeed, each ethical problem is projected onto it to generate an infinite recipe book. And another characteristic that makes it very flexible, much more than a simple recipe, is the feedback inherent to it. There's clearly a loop in the form of dialogue, but there's another loop hidden in the continuous use of the criterion in an endless series of situations. When we reach the end, we have new information we can use to start the process again from the beginning. This global iteration causes the entire community to converge toward the same objective before a decision can be made.

XARGOS.— We've established absolute relativism.

MARA.— What?

XARGOS.— Yes. Given a specific problem, the criterion will always produce the same result, right?

HERMES.— As long as we have the right information for that purpose. Remember the need for proper education.

XARGOS.— Right. So, except for that pitfall, the answer to a given problem is universal; it's absolute. But if we change the problem, we'll get a different answer. The appropriate solution to each specific problem will differ from one problem to another. In this sense, the answer is relative. That's why I alluded to absolute relativism.

HERMES.— What a curious approach. If we focus on its absolute nature, we can establish an absolute definition of happiness, unhappiness and indifference.

Let's accept the following definition: the result of an action permitted by the Criterion is happiness. The result of an incorrect action is unhappiness. Where the Criterion cannot distinguish between correct and incorrect actions, the result is indifference. Once this definition is established, the 'happy medium' determined by the Criterion is relative because it depends on each specific problem.

MARA.— I like this approach. It couldn't happen any other way. One is virtuous not when one acts in the same way just because, or because it once worked, but when one acts rightly on each occasion. To each situation, an approach. To each problem, a solution.

XARGOS.— What is the approach we're following? Is it the same approach any other person would follow in this same instant to respond to our initial question?

HERMES.— The enemy in this undertaking is the Universe itself, which will undoubtedly result in failures due to the magnitude of the adversary. These failures could produce a feeling of powerlessness, so common to everyday living, or a desire for self-improvement. People will try to push aside the feelings of powerlessness arising from frustration in order to seek the challenge, or the goal to be reached, in this natural order. The effort required for a successful campaign against the natural order will lead them to establish an action criterion that will enable them to distinguish good actions from bad ones. The good actions will take them closer to order, and therefore happiness, and the bad actions will take them farther away from happiness.

At this instant, I do believe that this approach is universal.

XARGOS.— It will be universal as long as a consensus is reached. What exactly does dialogue involve?

HERMES.— That's a tremendous question that would require an extensive discussion, but I think we can define it for this context. To engage in dialogue is to use language as a tool for establishing a common procedure to take us closer to order and farther from disorder, closer to happiness and farther from unhappiness.

XARGOS.— In our dialogue, we deduced that one should not be passive if one wants to be happy. That's why we have proverbs such as 'He that would have the fruit must climb the tree'.

MARA.— Interesting. Now I can certainly see that the criterion is a recipe book.

HERMES.— Things are ordered by making an effort or consuming some resources, either to achieve order or to maintain it. A quick conclusion we can draw from this action criterion is that the action requiring the least effort will probably lead to disorder, and therefore to unhappiness. So, decisions involving less effort can be dangerous. Beware of feelings of envy, revenge, fighting, or anger.

XARGOS.— That's why we have expressions like 'Behind the gentle barb lies the deadly barb', 'Good is the fight that is won, but better is the fight avoided',

'Open your eyes and you'll avoid anger', and 'Jealousy and envy take man's life away'.

The Universe

XARGOS.— We seem to have discovered that the Universe is bad.

HERMES.— What?

XARGOS.— It's bad because it tends to make us unhappy. Didn't we say that the Universe's natural tendency is toward disorder, which is bad because it leads to unhappiness?

HERMES.— Yes, we could summarise part of what we said that way, but we should qualify it.

XARGOS.— It seems obvious: it's bad.

HERMES.— Let's proceed carefully. It's not really good or bad per se. The Universe only acquires those labels because we're here to judge it. Goodness and badness are not qualities of the Universe; they only seem to be when humans make a mistake and label it as such. Humans are ethical, not the Universe It is humankind, a part of the Universe, who judges the goodness or badness of the Universe in its entirety. It makes no sense for an ethical being such as Xargos to consider the entire Universe as ethical. That would be as absurd as saying that the Universe has two arms, two legs, and a head joined to a trunk.

XARGOS.— I'm attributing qualities to the Universe that are not necessary for our reasoning, right?

HERMES.— That's right. The entire ethic we've built is essentially upheld by three pillars: the idea that order is a special way of doing things; that disorder leads to unhappiness; and that the Universe, in its way of doing things, knows nothing of order and disorder, happiness and unhappiness, and therefore evolves oblivious to the ethical problems of humankind. This last point is what prevents us from speaking of the goodness or badness of the Universe. Given that the dynamics of the Universe have nothing to do with our desires, hopes or ethical problems, we view its evolution as a natural law that tends to modify the order created by human beings and, in our view, turn it into disorder.

XARGOS.— So, the Universe only leads to disorder because it interferes with our order. If we weren't here, the evolution of the Universe would lack order and disorder. It would simply be what it has to be.

HERMES.— A vase is neither order nor disorder for the Universe. It will alter it in accordance with the laws governing its operation, but will not target it just because a vase might be more or less ordered than something else in our eyes. It is humankind who might regard the vase as more ordered because it provides a special way of doing things: it enables us to carry or store water, or simply decorate our workspace with the festive colours of a bouquet of flowers.

XARGOS.— In this last case, the special way of doing things would be…

HERMES.— …working gladly in a more pleasant space.

XARGOS.— In no way does the Universe tend to move toward disorder; it simply evolves. Humans can make judgments after observing that as the Universe evolves, it alters and therefore destroys those paths we created, with effort, for having different special ways of doing things. Because humans exist, the judgments we make also exist. And because it is humankind who talks about the Universe, we can summarise our relationship with it as follows: the Universe tends to disorder what I previously ordered. I can therefore establish that the Universe's tendency with regard to everything that interests me is that it tends to move toward disorder.

HERMES.— That's right. The Universe would be bad if it operated intentionally to hurt us by introducing disorder into those things we need. However, it's not the Universe's will to function that way; it's merely its only way of being. It introduces disorder simply because what we call order is the prior situation.

MARA.— To create order, all that is needed is to produce a differentiation with respect to the environment at some point, so that things are not homogeneous. One of the most interesting differentiations is life.

HERMES.— In a broad sense, we understand life to mean the duration of things. It is a colloquial reflection of our common sense: all things tend to lose the harmony that characterises them, and therefore disappear as such. In other words, their lives end.

XARGOS.— Life also differentiates between animate and inanimate objects, or those that act and those that do not. That's why when someone loses their life, it's because the duration of the attribute that most identified them has ended: being alive, being able to act in their own way.

HERMES.— After so many centuries of talking about life, we're using the same word to describe its two main characteristics. First, whoever is capable of acting has life because they can prolong it or extinguish it. And second, everything has a duration, and is perishable, extinguishable, and subject to the natural order. In other words, no attribute characteristic of anything is eternal.

Love

XARGOS.— It turns out that we are sentimental beings. The Imperative is not sentimental at all. Empathy, emotion and love are not properties that accompany it. How does such a physical, rigorous and apparently cold world fit into the warm context of human relationships?

MARA.— The Criterion obviously doesn't possess human qualities: it doesn't feel or suffer, it isn't affectionate, and it doesn't love. It is the person using it who loves. What is love?

HERMES.— It's a feeling that moves one to wish that the loved reality, another person, a group of people, or a thing, will attain what is judged to be its good; to strive so that this desire is fulfilled; and to enjoy its fulfilment as if it were our own good. It's also the care with which one works on something, delighting in it.

MARA.— The criterion seeks the good, or happiness, of everyone involved in the objectives. It does this through dialogue and through its method of detecting disorder. It incites the people questioning it to use it, and strives to meet the previous premise. It is a method requiring effort, and must therefore be used with care. Every step must be meditated and enjoyed along the way, until we know that what we're doing is to achieve a common good. That, for me, is Love.

HERMES.— Excellent comparison. The criterion is so similar to love, according to the drastically abbreviated definition we're using, that the former could almost be used to define the latter. Thus, someone who doesn't love won't be able to use the criterion in its entirety. By the same token, someone who doesn't understand the scope of the criterion will have difficulties loving. I would venture to say that a deep understanding of the criterion leads to love.

XARGOS.— So, if the criterion leads to love, that's because love is something good, it's right, and it's the path we should follow?

HERMES.— That seems to be the case.

MARA.— Suppose I'm considering whether I should love in order to be happy.

HERMES.— We know we have to act in order to be happy, and love is a possible action for achieving this. A better approach, as we've seen, would be to establish a more specific objective: I wish to be happy, and am therefore considering making others happy. The action I choose is to love them. Should I do it?

XARGOS.— So, by loving them, you wish for those fortunate souls for whom you profess your love to receive what is good for them. In order to discover what is good for them, you'll have to engage in a dialogue to determine what objective to wish for. When this coincides with your desire, you'll undertake any action leading to that objective that's in your hands. Loving means successfully achieving what I just described. This will undoubtedly require an effort. The opposite action is therefore to not investigate the desires of others, to not find out what would make them happy, to not take any action to get it for them, and to not consider anyone. In other words, to not seek any good for them, but no bad either, because we have to choose the most efficient of the possible opposite actions. Thus, to love requires an effort, and not to love requires no effort. Because we have to choose the action requiring more effort, loving is the right action!

MARA.— So, if loving is the right thing to do, we have to do it always, and the very best we can. 'Love thy neighbour as thyself!' is a statement that fits in perfectly with our arguments.

Part IV

Sustainability

Sustainability

Summary

Ethics tells us what is right and what is wrong. In particular, it tells us what actions are correct, and what actions are incorrect. It serves as a guide, or criterion, to help us determine what action to take. The chapter *Reflections of an excursionist* describes the ingredients of the ethic and moral criterion introduced in this book. This chapter shows how they relate to sustainability. As a result, it contains concepts such as environment, effort, efficiency, conflict, finiteness, fuzziness, extinction, and sustainability.

Definition of environment

An action, for example *do*, transforms certain attributes or specific characteristics of an object or set of entities, resulting in other attributes for the same object or set of entities. *A* is the initial set of attributes before performing the action, and *B* is the final set of attributes after performing the action. We can say that set *B* is set *A* transformed. The attributes contained in set *B* are those directly related to the purpose of the *do* action. In other words, the attributes obtained by transforming *A*, contained in set *B*, are the raison d'être of the *do* action; they describe the objective to be met. The *undo* action is the one that changes the final attributes contained in set *B* back into the initial attributes contained in set *A*. Note that we define the *undo* action using only sets *A* and *B*, regardless of the nature of the action. It is important to remember that throughout this chapter, the items in sets *A* and *B* are attributes of objects, not the objects themselves.

To *do* is to perform an action that transforms *A* into *B*. Because *A* and *B* only include those attributes related to the objective of the action, they do not contain all attributes that describe the objects involved. Thus, all attributes not included in *A* that are necessary to explain its evolution, to recount how the action was performed, or to describe the objects involved, constitute the *environment of A*. We can therefore define the *environment of A* as the set that complements *A* until both form a set of attributes sufficiently isolated from everything they do not include. Similarly, the set of all attributes not contained in *B* that are necessary to explain the evolution of *B* constitute the *environment of B*. Note that the elements in sets *A* and *B* are attributes that will have certain defined values or characteristics. There will be situations where certain attributes of an object belong to set *A*, and other attributes of the same object belong to the *environment of A*. There will be other situations where all attributes of an object belong to either set *A* or its environment. The same thing can happen to set *A* after it has been transformed. During the transformation of *A* into *B*, the environment of *A* interacts with *A* until it becomes the environment of *B* and *B*, respectively. By definition, during the transformation of *A* into *B*, the associated environment is sufficiently isolated from any other entity not included in *B*, *A* or itself.

For example, the action do= "*build a dike with turbines to harness the force of the tide*" transforms attribute *A*={*level equal to sea level*} of a volume of water into *B*={*level different from sea level*}. In this case, a possible *undo* action could be *build gates in the dike* (because evening out the water levels transforms *B* into *A*). Another possible *undo* action could be *demolish the dike*. The environment of *A* (or *B*) contains attributes not directly involved in the objective of the action for the water {*evaporation rate, marine currents, salinity, temperature, luminosity, life forms, etc.*} and for the coastline and sea bed {*beauty, geometry, materials, etc.*} Skill and knowledge are required to choose the attributes of the environment in order to make it a sufficiently isolated set.

Definition of way of doing things

A way of doing things is a procedure, or set of activities, that transforms one set of attributes into another set of attributes. The *do* action is a way of doing things that transforms set *A* into set *B*. The *undo* action is a way of doing things that transforms set *B* into set *A*. Actions are therefore ways of doing things.

In a general case, there are many possible actions for both doing and undoing. The *potential do actions* are the set of all actions that take set *A* and transform it into set *B*. The *potential undo actions* are the set of all actions that take set *B* and turn it back into set *A*.

This process is shown in Figure 1. On the diagram, each different action is identified with a number. The actions in the set of potential do actions appear as i=1,2,3,…, and those in the set of potential undo actions are shown as j=1,2,3,…. The number of actions in both sets does not necessarily have to coincide, and does not have to be finite or numerable. (Nevertheless, in this chapter they are assumed to be numerable for the sake of simplicity.) Because both do_i, which transforms *A* into *B*, and $undo_j$, which transforms *B* into *A*, are actions, we'll use the following nomenclature: $do_i = a(A,B;i)$ and $undo_j = a(B,A;j)$. The advantage of this nomenclature is that it specifies the initial and final sets involved in each action.

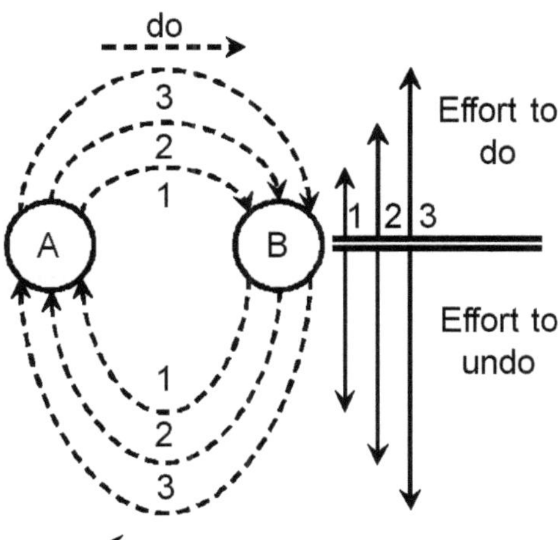

Figure 1 The *do* and *undo* actions acting on sets *A* and *B*.

Definition of effort

Each action contained in a set of potential actions is assigned a measure of the effort required to perform it. Effort quantifies how difficult it is to carry out the action. It includes concepts such as difficulty, complexity, resource consumption, time, people involved, etc., required to perform the action. For example, when one action involves more difficulty than another, we say that it requires more effort. Thus, as it becomes more difficult to transform *A* into *B*, the effort required to perform the action increases. We say that the effort required is infinite when the difficulty is of such magnitude that the action is unviable. We can do the same with the complexity, resources, time, etc. By definition, two actions requiring different amounts of effort are different.

By convention, we list all actions by increasing order of effort. Thus, the effort required for the action do_i, which turns *A* into *B*, is less than that required for the action do_{i+1}, which turns *A* into *B*. This allows us to use the numbers identifying the different actions, i=1,2,3,..., to indicate the effort required for each one. In other words, the amount of effort associated with each action establishes a relationship of order between the actions sharing the same initial and final sets. For a set of potential actions, this relationship of order is: $a(A,B;1) < a(A,B;2) < a(A,B;3) < \ldots$ Thus, the action requiring the least amount of effort is 1, and there is no other action that turns *A* into *B* with less effort. In addition, if *A* is the set, of all the possible initial sets, that enables us to obtain *B* with the least effort, then there is no action other than $a(A,B;1)$ for obtaining *B* with less effort. Action number 2 requires an intermediate amount of effort with respect to 1 and 3, and so on.

The length of the arrows shown on the right side of Fig. 1 represents the measure of the effort required to perform the *do* or *undo* actions between two sets, *A* and *B*. In the particular case shown, the effort required to undo exceeds the effort required to do, but there can be situations where more effort is required to do than to undo.

Relationship between effort and environment

If set *A* remains identical to itself for a given period of time, the most efficient action for preserving *A* is to *wait* because it consumes no resources. Thus, *wait* is action $a(A,A;1)$. On the other hand, the evolution of set *A* can be altered voluntarily. For example, we can recover set *A* after going through set *B*. To do so, we can perform undo action $a(B,A;1)$ after do action $a(A,B;1)$. It is obvious that performing these actions consecutively will require more effort than waiting and not doing anything. The sequence of actions therefore meets $[a(A,B;1) \rightarrow a(B,A;1)] > a(A,A;1)$. Thus, we have found an action that transforms *A* into *A* and requires more effort than $a(A,A;1)$. We can call the new action $a(A,A;2) = [a(A,B;1) \rightarrow a(B,A;1)]$. Both actions require different amounts of effort, and are therefore different. Because both actions share the same initial and final sets, but are different actions, the only possibility is that the final environment will be different for each one. In other words, the environment of A evolves differently if we apply action $a(A,A;2)$

than if we apply $a(A,A;1)$. Because action $a(A,A;1)$ simply involves waiting without interacting with set A, we can assume that if the elapsed time is short enough, the environment of A will not evolve, and will remain identical to itself. We can therefore conclude that the greater effort required to apply action $a(A,A;2)$ resulted in a greater transformation of the environment. The more effort is devoted to ensuring the maintenance of set A, the greater the impact on the environment will be. The more inefficient the action used to preserve the initial set of attributes, the greater the transformation of the environment.

Figure 2 shows the effects on the environment of choosing one action or the other. Note that, in general, the environment obtained after the undo action does not match the initial environment. This is indicated on the diagram with increasingly dark shading. This figure generalises Fig. 1, which showed the elements involved in the *do* and *undo* actions independently of the environment.

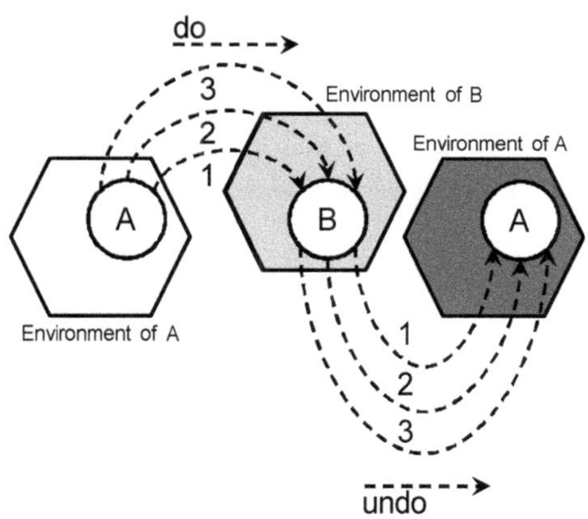

Figure 2 Effects of the *do* and *undo* actions on the environment of *A*.

The above idea leads us to the following generalisation. We can postulate that in a set of potential actions, two actions are different if, and only if, they transform the environment differently. The difference in effort also influences to what extent the environment is transformed. The environment of B is different if we apply $a(A,B;1)$ or $a(A,B;2)$.

Evolution of the environment

We now postulate that if a set is sufficiently isolated, its evolution, whatever that may be, always reduces the available number of ways of doing things contained in the set. This postulate is the result of an abstraction from nature. Note that we introduce the concept *sufficiently isolated* because we assume that there is no way to achieve perfect isolation. Assessing whether the degree of isolation is sufficient for predicting whether the evolution of the environment will destroy ways of doing things is a difficult task. This will lead to conflicts of assessment, finiteness and sustainability, which will be discussed later.

By definition, we said that set A and its environment must constitute a sufficiently isolated set. Thus, regardless of the A and B sets chosen, all potential *do* actions for turning A into B will reduce the number of ways of doing things present in the set comprised of A and its environment. This is true as long as the environment meets the condition of being a sufficiently isolated set, regardless of whether B contains a higher or lower number of ways of doing things than A. If a set does not meet the condition of being sufficiently isolated, it does not necessarily reduce the number of ways of doing things. For example, we know that set A is not sufficiently isolated from its environment. Set A could therefore increase or decrease the number of ways of doing things.

Ethical framework

Ethically correct actions are those that create new ways of doing things, while keeping the decrease in the number of ways of doing things to a minimum.

Moral criterion

As we saw, there is an ethical principle that enables us to distinguish right from wrong and make decisions by evaluating the effort associated with two actions: the *do* action and the *undo* action. The correctness of the action is deduced by comparing the minimum effort associated with *do* to the minimum effort associated with *undo*.

This moral criterion requires us to consider all possible sets of actions that start with different A sets and always end with the same B set. The A set eventually chosen to identify what is right, i.e., to apply the moral criterion, will be the one that enables us to perform the *do* action with the least possible effort. Thus, the criterion says that actions $a(A,B;i)$ and $a(B,A;i)$ with $i>1$ are always incorrect. The moral criterion also indicates that action $a(A,B;1)$ is correct if it requires greater effort than $a(B,A;1)$, i.e., if $a(A,B;1)> a(B,A;1)$. If $a(A,B;1)\leq a(B,A;1)$, then action $a(A,B;1)$ is incorrect. The general form of the moral criterion is:

'Let A_α be the different initial sets that can be transformed into the same final B set. Here, α is a label that covers a complete and appropriate set of indices (for example, $\alpha\in[0,\infty)$, $\alpha =1,2,3,\ldots$). Let $a(A_\alpha,B;i)$ with i=1,2,3… be the different actions, ordered from lesser to greater effort, that transform the A_α sets into B. Let A be the set that verifies $a(A,B;1)\leq a(A_\alpha,B;i)$ for all values of α and i. Thus, the moral criterion states that:

All actions different from $a(A,B;1)$ or $a(B,A;1)$ are always incorrect. (In particular, actions $a(A_\alpha,B;i)$ and $a(B,A_\alpha;i)$ with $i>1$ are incorrect for any value of alpha.) If $a(A,B;1)>a(B,A;1)$, then action $a(A,B;1)$ is correct. Otherwise, it is incorrect.'

If a transformation of set *A* is correct according to the above moral criterion, we can postulate that set *B*, transformed from *A*, allows for a larger number of ways of doing things than *A*. We can also postulate that the environment of *B* contains fewer ways of doing things than the environment of *A*. These ethical postulates, like the moral criterion presented, are abstracted from observations of the physical world.

If transforming *A* into *B* is a correct action, then *B* is more ordered than *A* because it allows for more ways of doing things. If transforming *A* into *B* is a correct action, then the environment of *B* is less ordered than *A*.

Ethical definition of order

By definition, we say that one situation is more ordered than another if, and only if, it contains a larger number of ways of doing things.

Ethical definition of happiness

We define happiness as that situation where there is a sufficient number of correct ways of doing things. Thus, the greater the order, the greater the possibility of being happy.

Ethics as a conflict of interests

To lose possible actions in either the present or the future is to lose ways of doing things. Consequently, to lose actions is to lose order and happiness.

Actions cease to be available if the initial set disappears, or if they are no longer correct. In addition, because the final set for one action might be the initial set for another, if the final set for one action disappears, actions will also disappear. Each time an action reduces the set of available attributes or the set of correct actions available, there will be a conflict of interest. These conflicts arise from the loss of ways of doing things. A conflict will be produced if performing one action alters the initial set affected by another action, the final set generated, or its ethical assessment.

In general, in the context of this book, a conflict is a situation where the ethical assessment of an action can produce contradictory tendencies or results.

Scarcity, interference and environmental conflicts

Let α and β be two individuals (or entities). Individual α transforms set A_α into B_α, while individual β transforms set A_β into B_β.

Performing $a(A_\alpha,B_\alpha;1)$ can make it difficult or impossible to perform $a(A_\beta,B_\beta;1)$. This might be because:

1) The use of A_α destroys or modifies set A_β (scarcity conflict).
2) Transforming A_β into B_β destroys or modifies set B_α (interference conflict).
3) Transforming A_α into B_α destroys or modifies set A_β (environmental conflict).

This last type of conflict occurs because action $a(A_\alpha,B_\alpha;1)$ inevitably transforms the environment of A_α, where A_β is located, into the environment of B_α, where A_β might no longer be.

Thus, when sets A_α and A_β are not disjoint, a scarcity conflict arises. When B_α and B_β are not disjoint, an interference conflict arises. When A_α and A_β are disjoint, and B_α and B_β are also disjoint, an environmental conflict may arise. This may occur even if actions $a(A_\alpha,B_\alpha;1)$ and $a(A_\beta,B_\beta;1)$, considered independently from each other, are correct.

The assessment conflict

In general, actions $a(A_\alpha,B_\alpha;1)$ and $a(A_\beta,B_\beta;1)$ might facilitate or hinder each other even if none of the above conflicts exist between them. For example, after performing action $a(A_\alpha,B_\alpha;1)$, action $a(A_\beta,B_\beta;1)$ might no longer require the minimum effort.

In fact, when there are no scarcity, interference or environmental conflicts, performing action $a(A_\alpha,B_\alpha;1)$ might modify the ethical assessment of action $a(A_\beta,B_\beta;1)$. In other words, the efforts associated with the *do* and *undo* actions change, along with the ethical assessment of the transformation, even though sets A_β and B_β do not change. This might happen if:

1) Action $a(A_\alpha,B_\alpha;1)$ results in new ways of transforming A_β into B_β, or the existing ones are modified or eliminated.
2) New ways of transforming B_β into A_β are produced, or the existing ones are modified or eliminated.

If we use an asterisk to identify the new actions associated with these new ways of doing things, we'll have the following relationships of order: $a^*(A_\beta,B_\beta;1) < a^*(A_\beta,B_\beta;2) < a^*(A_\beta,B_\beta;3) < \ldots$ and $a^*(B_\beta,A_\beta;1) < a^*(B_\beta,A_\beta;2) < a^*(B_\beta,A_\beta;3) < \ldots$. With these new actions, the feasible cases are:

1) $a^*(A_\beta,B_\beta;1) < a^*(B_\beta,A_\beta;1)$. In other words, $a(A_\alpha,B_\alpha;1)$ makes the later transformation of A_β into B_β incorrect.
2) $a^*(A_\beta,B_\beta;1) > a^*(B_\beta,A_\beta;1)$, but $a^*(A_\beta,B_\beta;1) > a(A_\beta,B_\beta;1)$. In other words, the later transformation of A_β into B_β is correct, but more inefficient than before performing $a(A_\alpha,B_\alpha;1)$.
3) $a^*(A_\beta,B_\beta;1) > a^*(B_\beta,A_\beta;1)$, but $a^*(A_\beta,B_\beta;1) < a(A_\beta,B_\beta;1)$. In other words, the later transformation of A_β into B_β is correct and more efficient.

Suppose that actions $a(A_\alpha,B_\alpha;1)$ and $a(A_\beta,B_\beta;1)$, considered independently of each other, are correct. Because action $a(A_\alpha,B_\alpha;1)$ is correct, we know that B_α contains a larger number of ways of doing things than A_α. However, the environment of B_α, where A_β is located, will have reduced the total number. Nevertheless, although the total number has decreased, the number of available ways of transforming A_β into B_β may have increased or decreased. The same is true of the number of ways of transforming B_β into A_β. Thus, the ethical assessment of action $a(A_\beta,B_\beta;1)$ could change from correct to incorrect (or vice-versa, if it was assumed to be incorrect).

The extinction conflict

We will now prove that to allow the extinction of a species (such as red tuna) or object (such as petroleum) is a morally incorrect action. To do so, we will analyse the extinction of A as follows. If, as a result of doing nothing, set A is going to become extinct in order to become set B_α, the action *wait* (associated with not taking any preventive measures) involves zero effort. However, the *undo* action that fights against A becoming B_α requires planning, resources, and effort for transforming B_α back into A. Therefore, $a(A,B_\alpha;1) < a(B_\alpha,A;1)$ is true, and the action *wait* is incorrect. To not promote actions to prevent the extinction of a species is an ethically incorrect action.

Note that with the extinction of A, all actions that could transform A into anything else are lost. Because actions are ways of doing things, by losing A we lose all actions originating from it. Along with those actions, we lose order and, quite possibly, happiness. This loss will have repercussions from the moment of extinction into the future. For example, transforming A into a B_β set other than B_α could be of interest at some point. However, if A has become extinct, this correct way of obtaining B_β will have disappeared.

If A becomes extinct as a result of an action, a new conflict arises, which we'll call an extinction conflict. This conflict occurs when we recognise that the future possibility of transforming A into B_β is lost if A has disappeared. This conflict is even more severe if the lost action, $a(A,B_\beta;1)$, was correct. Resolving such conflict is even more complex if the extinction of A is not the result of an incorrect action,

$a(A,B_\alpha;1) < a(B_\alpha,A;1)$, but of a correct action, $a(A,B_\alpha;1) > a(B_\alpha,A;1)$. This is the case even though B_α contains more ways of doing things than A, because the extinction of A completely eliminates all ways of doing things associated with A from the present to the future.

The extinction conflict is intimately related to the scarcity conflict. It can be considered an extreme case in which the scarcity of resource A becomes maximal and permanent. Scarcity and extinction can be caused by correct resource use, but can also occur due to the natural evolution of resources. Note that the moral criterion avoids incorrect resource use.

The finiteness conflict

Trying to eliminate or minimise the conflicts described above results in a new kind of conflict: the finiteness conflict. To examine it, let's consider the interference conflict, which must be avoided because it's highly inefficient. When it happens, it consumes resources to destroy the result of a previous action that was also performed by consuming resources. However, in addition to increasing the inefficiency, the interference conflict can also lead to incorrect ethical assessments. To explore this, let's assume that someone has decided that action $a(B_\alpha,A_\alpha;1)$ is correct, i.e., $a(B_\alpha,A_\alpha;1) > a(A_\alpha,B_\alpha;1)$, and is therefore undertaking that action. Now someone else wants to execute action $a(A_\alpha,B_\alpha;1)$, but is completely unaware that the first person is performing action $a(B_\alpha,A_\alpha;1)$. When the second person assesses the action for transforming A_α into B_α, they'll get action $a(A_\alpha,B_\alpha;1)$, and when they assess the *undo* action for transforming B_α into A_α, they'll get $a^*(B_\alpha,A_\alpha;1)$. This requires much less effort than action $a(B_\alpha,A_\alpha;1)$ because it's already being executed, even though they don't know who or what is doing it. They'll find that the undo action is 'free'. Thus, they'll discover that $a(A_\alpha,B_\alpha;1) > a^*(B_\alpha,A_\alpha;1)$. Action $a(A_\alpha,B_\alpha;1)$ is therefore correct, and they'll begin to execute it. This will increase the effort the first person must expend to eliminate B_α. After applying the criterion, they'll find even greater reason to perform the action. This upward spiral of resource consumption can end in any situation: where A_α prevails over B_α, B_α prevails over A_α, or A_α and B_α coexist in a dynamic equilibrium that will eventually end in one of the two situations mentioned above. An observer, who is aware of the existence of both characters and regards them as one, will see that both are performing action a^* on set $A_\alpha \cup B_\alpha$, and the result is either mostly A_α, or mostly B_α. Due to the interference conflict, $a^*(A_\alpha \cup B_\alpha,B_\alpha;1) > a(A_\alpha,B_\alpha;1)$ or $a^*(A_\alpha \cup B_\alpha,A_\alpha;1) > a(B_\alpha,A_\alpha;1)$ will verify. He therefore finds an action that produces the same result, but with less effort than the action used. This indicates that action $a^*(A_\alpha \cup B_\alpha,B_\alpha;1)$ could not be the first on the ordered list. This external observer therefore concludes that action $a^*(A_\alpha \cup B_\alpha,B_\alpha;1)$ is incorrect. This is the logical result of the efficiency imposed by the proposed moral criterion.

Thus, being unaware that someone or something else is undertaking actions that affect our actions can lead to false ethical assessments. To avoid this, we must be aware of each and every one of the actions being performed, and the network of sets connecting them. The set containing all the actions must include all entities (both animate and inanimate) in the environment of our action, and in the sets affected by it. We must therefore know how to define the environment, to ensure that it's sufficiently isolated, as well as the affected attributes. We are also required to know all sets of potential do and undo actions, which includes knowing how to measure and assess the efforts required. It also involves knowing how each one affects the environment, in addition to any present or future actions that might be performed by third parties. This enormous amount of information exceeds the amount manageable for a single human being. The finiteness of a human being therefore makes a proper ethical assessment of all actions unviable. Due to finiteness, a correct action for an individual might not be right for a group. We call this kind of conflict a finiteness conflict.

Global scope of the proposed ethic

Although the moral criterion presented here can be applied by a single individual making personal decisions, the previous point warns of the risk that person would be taking. Except for highly simplified particular cases, the moral criterion presented is a global criterion that should be applied with an awareness of the activities of all other beings acting on the planet. Otherwise, the conflicts described above will arise, and with them a lack of moral continuity: we won't find morally correct actions that produce correct actions in the future. This means that all actions undertaken on Earth influence both present and future ethical decision-making. And this is true regardless of who is performing the action: a plant, animal, another person, a group of people, a country, an organisation, or the planet itself through the climate, the tides, etc.

The proposed ethic is global, both spatially and temporally, because it includes all entities and all individuals in both present and future generations. The planet and all beings on it have intrinsic ethical value.

Globality and fuzziness

To regard an action as correct based on partial or incomplete information is very risky. For example, even if the criterion views the transformation of set *A* into set *B* as correct, the environment is also transformed. As a result of that transformation, different ways of doing things can disappear, which are unrecoverable or very difficult to recover due to their special nature. Not knowing that another being is undertaking actions that affect our actions, or that our actions are affecting those of other entities, also generates conflicts, inefficiency, and false ethical assessments. It is therefore advisable to provide the necessary means to increase transparency, information, participation, dialogue, etc.

Thus, when we make it our objective to increase the number of ways of doing things and apply the moral criterion to see whether those actions are correct, dialogue and study are absolutely necessary. Dialogue is needed to learn about other people's activities, and study to learn about the present and future activities of all other entities. Study is also required to learn about the greatest possible number of ways of doing things, and the associated efforts. Such dialogue and study must be universal and completely transversal. They would therefore be homogeneous among all individuals, and there would be no doubt about their scope.

All people must therefore be interested in the result, both present and future, of the ethical decision. To participate, we are all required to acknowledge the other parties involved as valid interlocutors for the purpose of setting a common objective and collecting the information required to properly apply the moral criterion. For everyone to know what the relevant information is, everyone must have access to the previously handled information: the participation process must be undertaken with maximum transparency. In addition, as required by the moral criterion, such participation must be as efficient as possible.

The proposed ethic suggests that sustainability is achieved when the entire society adopts the moral criterion, and its underlying ethic, as an obligation. Implicit in this obligation is the result of the ethic itself and its moral criterion: it is correct to increase efficiency by reducing the misuse of resources, and to act to increase the number of available ways of doing things by selecting the correct actions through the global application of the proposed moral criterion.

The finiteness of human beings, both individually and collectively, makes it impossible for us to have a permanent, homogeneous, full and complete capacity for dialogue and study, and makes the participation of all individuals and the information handled partial, distorted, incomplete, and unclear. This is why the knowledge available for making ethical assessments of humans as a species is fuzzy, much more so for individuals than for the species. Globality implies fuzziness. This is due to the finiteness conflict, and must be taken as a fact. The moral criterion presented seeks to increase the number of ways of doing things, and will thereby facilitate dialogue, study, and the flow of information, and gradually turn fuzziness into clarity. A correct approach to globality means reducing fuzziness.

Definition of sustainability

Sustainability means to increase the number of ways of doing things without decreasing the number of existing ones.

This definition means that future generations will find increasing amounts of order, and consequently, a greater possibility of happiness.

The moral criterion that enables us to keep humankind within this ethical framework is based on the idea that the correct action is the one that allows us the greatest number of ways of doing things in the future.

Sustainability is therefore an ethical principle.

The sustainability conflict

It is interesting to note that if fuzziness were completely eliminated, and all of the conflicts described above were avoided, there is a final conflict whose effect can be minimised, but never eliminated. This conflict can be stated as follows: in a sufficiently isolated set, sustainability is unachievable.

The sustainability conflict is intimately related to the assessment and environmental conflicts, but a new nuance is added: our actions on a sufficiently isolated system accelerate global disorder. Indeed, every transformation of an isolated system reduces the number of ways of doing things available in that system. The greater the effort expended in the transformation, the more ways of doing things will be eliminated. In addition, creating new ones requires selecting those actions that verify $a(A,B;1) > a(B,A;1)$, where the correct action is to transform A into B, and not vice-versa. We can therefore deduce that creating new ways of doing things using $a(A,B;1)$ requires more effort than the $a(A,C;1)$ action associated with not creating them and allowing A to evolve freely for a long period. Consequently, the number of ways of doing things lost in the environment of A increases when $a(A,B;1)$ is performed. Because A and its environment are a sufficiently isolated set, their order will decrease regardless of the action performed: what we now know is that $a(A,B;1)$ accelerates the process of destroying ways of doing things. A new conflict therefore arises, which we'll call the sustainability conflict. In this conflict, the ethical correctness of the action does not change. Rather, a contradiction appears because we know we have to act to create the new ways of doing things granted by $a(A,B;1)$, and that this action will destroy ways available in the environment of C. This conflict is unsolvable as long as the environment is a sufficiently isolated system.

Fortunately, planet Earth is not a sufficiently isolated set: it relates to the outside through the exchange of particles, electromagnetic fields (mainly solar radiation), and gravitational fields (mainly those of the sun and moon). This relationship to the outside can enable planet Earth, set A, to order itself.

When we find a sufficiently isolated system within the planet, the above conflict arises, and ordering one part of the system necessarily disorders another part. For example, a sufficiently isolated container containing fuel and air can be transformed with relatively little effort into combustion products at a high temperature. All that is required is a simple spark caused by some impact and very little time. However, to synthesise fuel from the combustion products would require a very slow process in which a plant, capable of using sunlight to produce wood, would turn the carbon dioxide and water back into fuel. The size of the environment required in both cases is very disparate. In the first case, the environment is the stone used to make the spark and a bit of energy to move it. However, in the second case, the environment comprises the entire surroundings of the living being plus the required solar radiation. The second case requires more elements, more time, more difficulty, and therefore more effort. Thus, burning fuel is an incorrect action. However, until we can use solar energy or tidal power, burning fuel to produce high-quality materials is a correct action. (To ruin high-quality steel, all we would have to do would be to smelt it in an environment contaminated with impurities and cool it without any control.) The conflict lies in acknowledging that:

1) Using renewable energy for all activities is correct, and such energy must be used as soon as it's available.
2) However, to create the systems for generating renewable energy, we need tools, materials, etc., that had to be designed without such energy.

Knowing that the energy that should be used comes from the outside, and that in order to use it, we must first use sufficiently isolated systems, is a conflict that must be resolved. However, this conflict comes from knowing, as we have proven, that it is ethically correct to minimise the use of sufficiently isolated systems. (Note that to not minimise their use is ethically incorrect because it leads to scarcity and extinction conflicts.)

Value of the ethic

With the definitions given, the concept of sustainability falls well within the ethical framework and moral criterion presented. This is because all the definitions are linked by the number of available ways of doing things. We must not forget that happiness lies in having a sufficient number of ways of doing things.

- Ways of doing things are transformed by actions undertaken by living things and by the planet itself. Some actions will destroy them, while others will preserve and create them. The moral criterion presented maximises the maintenance and creation of ways of doing things, and minimises their destruction. The process also reinforces and sustains itself: the more ways there are to do things, the greater the possibility of finding morally correct actions. The ways available reside on the planet, which is why the entire planet has intrinsic ethical value. Resources, living beings, artificial artefacts, and ecosystems have both actual and potential ways of doing things in both the present and the future.

- In order for actions to be correct and also improve the efficiency of future actions, we need to eliminate scarcity, interference, environmental, extinction, assessment and finiteness conflicts, as well as the actions that increase the incorrectness or inefficiency of future actions. The moral criterion itself reduces fuzziness by increasing the number of available ways of reducing conflicts, and therefore leads to clarity in its global application.
- This necessarily promotes participation, dialogue, and study as ethically correct actions. It therefore leads us to refine the terms, concepts, postulates, arguments, and approaches required to build a consistent policy for the planet. Such a policy would be ethical, and therefore sustainable.
- It is fascinating to note that increasing the efficiency of present or future actions, if they are morally correct according to the criterion presented, increases both present and future happiness. Indeed, more efficiency means less effort to achieve the same degree of order. The present generation will therefore work less to achieve the same, or will work the same and achieve more. Thus, the future generation will either enjoy a greater available effort or a larger number of special ways of doing things, which will in turn result in greater efficiency. The inappropriate use of resources is a morally incorrect activity, and therefore reprehensible.
- In the current situation, climate change can lead to the extinction of many ecosystems. It is morally incorrect to wait for that to happen without doing anything. If something is potentially irreversible, it must be given priority in our ethical arguments. The extinction of species is of great ethical interest.
- Eliminating the sustainability conflict invites us to reduce the use of sufficiently isolated systems within the planet, and encourages us to replace them with the planet's external energy sources, such as solar energy and tidal power.
- We can also bring back the arguments used by Hermes, Xargos and Mara to say that the use of the proposed ethic leads to the cardinal virtues (prudence, justice, temperance and fortitude), and to compassion, solidarity, and love.

The evolution of a rational species is sustainable if it makes all of its decisions in accordance with the Universal Categorical Imperative: Create new ways of doing things without destroying the existing ones!

Related Reading

Aurifeille, J.M. (2011). *Globalisation, Governance and Ethics: New Managerial and Economics Insights.* Nova Science Pub Incorporated.

Baura, G.D. (2006). *Engineering Ethics: An Industrial Perspective.* Elsevier.

Becker, C.U. (2011). *Sustainability Ethics and Sustainability Research.* Springer.

Becker, C.U. (2012). *Sustainability Ethics and Sustainability Research,* Springer.

Benavides, Efrén Moreno. (2008). Ética Borrosa. Éride Ediciones and Luarna, Madrid, Spain.

Benavides, Efrén Moreno. (2009). Ética Borrosa. Luarna. Digital edition.

Bowers, J. (1997). *Sustainability and Environmental Economics: An Alternative Text.* Longman.

Brown, D. et al. (2007). White Paper on the Ethical Dimensions of Climate Change. Rock Ethics Institute at Pennsylvania State University, http://rockethics.psu.edu/climate/policy/edcc.shtml

Bunge, M. (1989). *Ethics: The Good and the Right.* D. Reidel Publishing Company.

Cairns, J. (2003). 'Eco-ethics and sustainability ethics'. Inter-Research.

Chick, A. & Micklethwaite, P. (2011). *Design for Sustainable Change: How Design and Designers Can Drive the Sustainability Agenda.* AVA Publishing.

Commission on Global Governance, The. (1995). *Our Global Neighbourhood.* Oxford University Press, Oxford.

Cooper, D. and Palmer, J.A., eds. (1992). *The Environment in Question: Ethics and Global Issues.* Routledge, London.

Des Jardins, J.R. (2006). *Environmental Ethics: An Introduction to Environmental Philosophy,* Wadsworth Publishing Co., Belmont, CA.

Dewall, W. & Sessions, G. (1995). *Deep Ecology: Living as if Nature Mattered.* Gibb M. Smith, Inc. Salt Lake City, UT.

Dobson, A. (1998). *Justice and the Environment: Conceptions of Environmental Sustainability and Theories of Distributive Justice.* Oxford University Press, Oxford.

Dower, N. (1997). *Development Issues: Environmental. The Encyclopedia of Applied Ethics* (ed. R. Chapman). Academic Press, New York.

Edwards, A. (2005). *The Sustainability Revolution: Portrait of a Paradigm Shift.* New Society Publishers, Philadelphia, PA

Engel, J.R. and Engel, J.G. (Eds.) (1990). *Ethics of Development and Environment: Global Challenge, International Responses.* Belhaven, New York.

Everett, B., Boyle, G. & Ramage, J. (2011). *Energy Systems and Sustainability: Power for a Sustainable Future.* Oxford University Press.

Fry, T. (2008). *Design Futuring: Sustainability, Ethics and New Practice.* Berg.

Held D. and Archibugi D. (Eds.) (1995). *Cosmopolitan Democracy: An Agenda for a New World Order.* Polity Press, Cambridge.

Humphreys, K.K. (1999). *What Every Engineer Should Know about Ethics.* Marcel Dekker, Inc.

Kibert, C.J., Thiele, L., Peterson, A. & Monroe, M. 'The ethics of sustainability.' Free PDF document.

Kierman, M.J. (2009). *Investing in a Sustainable World: Why GREEN Is the New Color of Money on Wall Street.* AMACOM Div. American Mgmt. Assn.

Nakata, S. (2005). *A House of Sustainability.* a+u Publishing Company.

Newton, L.H. (2003). *Ethics and Sustainability: Sustainable Development and the Moral Life.* Prentice Hall.

Redclift, M. (1989). *Sustainable Development: Exploring the Contradictions.* Routledge, London.

Russ, T.H. (2010). *Sustainability and Design Ethics.* CRC Press, Taylor & Francis Group.

Sandler, R. & Cafaro, P. (2005). *Environmental Virtue Ethics,* Rowman & Littlefield, Lanham, MD.

Schategger, S., Bennett, M. & Burrit, R. (Eds.) (2006). *Sustainability Accounting and Reporting.* Springer.

Scott, A. (1999). *Dimensions of Sustainability: Architecture, Form, Technology, Environment and Culture.* Taylor & Francis.

Sen, A.K. (1991). *On Ethics and Economics.* Blackwell.

Skirbekk, G. (Ed.) (1994). *The Notion of Sustainability and its Normative Implications.* Scandinavian University Press, Oslo.

Soverensen, S. (2009). *The Sustainable Network: The Accidental Answer for a Troubled Planet.* O'Reilly Media, Inc.

Spet, J.G. (2004). *Red Sky at Morning: America and the Crisis of the Global Environment.* Yale University Press, New Haven, CT.

Tencati, A., Perrini, F. (2011). *Business Ethics and Corporate Sustainability.* Edward Elgar Publishing.

Thompson, J. (1999). 'Planetary Citizen: In Defense of an Ideal.' *Government for the Environment: Global Problems, Ethics and Democracy.* (Eds. Low, N. & Gleeson, B.) Macmillan, London.

Uhl, C. (2004). *Developing Ecological Consciousness.* Rowman & Littlefield, Lanham, MD.

Whitbeck, C. (2011). *Ethics in Engineering Practice and Research.* Cambridge University Press.

Whiteside, K. (2006). *Precautionary Politics: Principle and Practice in Confronting Environmental Risk.* MIT Press, Cambridge, MA.

World Commission on Environment and Development. (1987). Our Common Future (Brundtland Report, 1987). Oxford, Oxford University Press.

Index

Page numbers followed by f indicate figures. Those followed by t indicate tables.

www.ingramcontent.com/pod-product-compliance
Ingram Content Group UK Ltd.
Pitfield, Milton Keynes, MK11 3LW, UK
UKHW020820290926
15470UKWH00003B/1264